BEGINNINGS
IN PSYCHOTHERAPY

BEGINNINGS IN PSYCHOTHERAPY
A Guidebook for New Therapists

Seth Eichler, M.D.

Taylor & Francis Group
LONDON AND NEW YORK

First published 2010 by
Karnac Books Ltd.

Published 2018 by Routledge
2 Park Square, Milton Park, Abingdon, Oxon OX14 4RN
711 Third Avenue, New York, NY 10017, USA

Routledge is an imprint of the Taylor & Francis Group, an informa business

Copyright © 2010 by Seth Eichler, M.D.

The right of Seth Eichler to be identified as the author of this work has been asserted in accordance with §§ 77 and 78 of the Copyright Design and Patents Act 1988.

All rights reserved. No part of this book may be reprinted or reproduced or utilised in any form or by any electronic, mechanical, or other means, now known or hereafter invented, including photocopying and recording, or in any information storage or retrieval system, without permission in writing from the publishers.

Notice:
Product or corporate names may be trademarks or registered trademarks, and are used only for identification and explanation without intent to infringe.

British Library Cataloguing in Publication Data

A C.I.P. for this book is available from the British Library

ISBN-13: 9781855758384 (pbk)

Typeset by Vikatan Publishing Solutions (P) Ltd., Chennai, India

To Barbara, Wendy, Jack, and Joanna
And to my parents, Robert and Anne Eichler

CONTENTS

ACKNOWLEDGEMENTS xi

SECTION I. EXPANDING MINDS: LEARNING
  TO THINK ANALYTICALLY 1
CHAPTER ONE
On beginnings 3

CHAPTER TWO
On meaning—understanding why we do what we do 7

CHAPTER THREE
On gratification and deprivation 11

SECTION II. TOOLS AND TECHNIQUES 15
CHAPTER FOUR
On regression and its use 17
- Insight-oriented versus supportive approach 19
- Transference 19
- Countertransference: Regression in the therapist 20

- Neutrality 21
- Safety and freedom 22
- Confidentiality 23
- Time: Frequency and timelessness 24
- Free association 25
- Silence 26
- Ambiguity 26
- The couch 28

CHAPTER FIVE
The frame 29
- Time 30
- The physical office 30
- Money 33
- Handling missed sessions 33

CHAPTER SIX
Creating a therapeutic atmosphere 35
- The therapeutic alliance 36

CHAPTER SEVEN
The consultation 39
- The analytic inquiry 41

SECTION III. GUIDEPOSTS FOR OUR WORK
IN LISTENING AND INTERVENING 43
CHAPTER EIGHT
Guideposts for our work in listening
and intervening 45
- Empathy 45
- Analytic listening 47
- Educating the patient 49
- Educating patients on their jobs 50
- Educating about cure: How treatment works 51
- On listening II: Learning to understand and cure 52
- On resistance 53
- Following the affect 54
- "Off-Key" notes 55

- Patterns 55
- Keeping self esteem in mind 56
- Going after pain 56
- Detective work 57
- The three areas of mental content 57
- Treatment as a listening focus 58
- Context and contiguity 58
- The lecture and the lab 59
- Intervening 61

SECTION IV: "OUR PATIENTS ARE OUR TEXTBOOKS":
LESSONS FROM CLINICAL CASES
(RAKO & MAZER, 1980) 65

CHAPTER NINE
Patient A.: Educating about cure 67
- The strands of the rope 72

CHAPTER TEN
Patient B.: Encouraging self-observation 75

CHAPTER ELEVEN
Patient C.: Identifying themes and furthering
understanding of how symptoms develop 81

CHAPTER TWELVE
Patient D.: Understanding the repetition compulsion
and unconscious fantasy 87
- Unconscious fantasy 89
- Working through 91

CHAPTER THIRTEEN
Patient E.: Giving patients new insights
about common themes 93
- Symptoms are fueled by gratification 96
- We work preconsciously 96

CHAPTER FOURTEEN
Patient F.: Working with dreams 99

SECTION V: CONCLUSION 113
CHAPTER FIFTEEN
On endings 115
- The room 116

BIBLIOGRAPHY 121

LYRIC ACKNOWLEDGMENT 123

INDEX 125

ACKNOWLEDGEMENTS

The sources of learning about psychotherapy are myriad. We draw on patients, teachers, supervisors, and authors, as well as our own therapists and analysts.

Far too many people have participated in the creation of this book for me to individually acknowledge, but I'd like to mention a few. Drs. Harold Blum, Robert Chalfin, Marianne Goldberger, David Newman, as well as the late Drs. Jules Glenn and Stephen Glick, all provided a great deal of help to me, each in their own unique way.

I'd like to thank everyone at Karnac Books as well as Lisa Tener who provided invaluable help in the process of editing.

My wife, Barbara, spent long hours reviewing and typing the manuscript. Her excellent ideas, as well as the enthusiastic support of my children, were important in making this possible. The unfailing encouragement from my parents has, as well, always been a source of great support.

Finally, my students over the years who encouraged me to write about what I was teaching were the impetus for this text.

SECTION I

EXPANDING MINDS: LEARNING TO THINK ANALYTICALLY

CHAPTER ONE

On beginnings

Psychotherapy has always been a passion for me. After twenty-seven years of practicing, I still feel passionately about it. I suspect that this is true for many therapists, including those who have been practicing longer than I have. Practicing psychotherapy is something I look forward to and, as I reflect on it, I find numerous parts of it I enjoy—sitting with people, learning about them, helping them, hearing about their lives, their pain, their victories. Perhaps most of all, I enjoy the feeling of understanding what's going on within them, and of having that understanding deepen over time.

Our field is a creative, rich, and exciting one. In a way, I can't imagine doing anything else. I find working with patients similar to reading great literature or watching a fine movie unfold. It is my wish that through this book you begin to appreciate and enjoy this rewarding endeavor.

There will always be a need for therapy and therapists, despite the allure of quick cures—including medication—that offer relief but don't deliver the benefits that psychotherapy can offer. These benefits include the feeling of being understood and the enormous comfort derived from having someone available who is consistently listening and present—a satisfaction that few other relationships provide. Additionally, it is gratifying for a patient who has been baffled by his or her symptoms finally being able to understand them. Recently a patient said to me, "I've never had someone really listen to me in my life before."

I wrote this book for beginning therapists who are just entering our field and for those thinking about becoming therapists. My intention has been that throughout this book, you will find a beginning framework for your work. As you understand certain important concepts, you will be able to facilitate the process of psychotherapy more knowledgeably and comfortably. I hope that you will learn what to listen for and how to hear it, in order to better understand the specifics of each patient's situation and needs.

Most beginning therapists want to help. We've all had our own pain and difficulties in life, and we want to help others with theirs. However well meaning our intentions, certain things that therapists do—and don't do—will influence, assist, and, sometimes, hinder patients from getting the kind of help they need. It is my hope that this book will provide you with a kind of map that allows you and your patient to get as far as you can (which can always be farther and farther).

Not everyone beginning to do this work will go on to have further training. For me, medical school wasn't enough, nor a psychiatric residency, nor a fellowship in psychotherapy. Through analytic training at NYU Medical Center—involving my own analysis, supervision, and course work—I gained a further understanding of why we're doing what we're doing. If this book whets a student's appetite to pursue further study, all the better. But all beginners need a place to begin. I remember as a medical student taking a psychiatry rotation and being told to go in and, "Just talk to the patient." I recall wondering, *Huh? What am I supposed to talk about?*

As a medical student and resident, I found that learning psychotherapy, and in particular, supervision, is a little like being told, "Go out, fly a plane, and we'll talk about it later" (Lewis, 1978, p. 4). This book has been written to teach you how to get the plane into the air, fly it, and prevent crash landings. As time goes on, your experience in sitting with patients will make you more comfortable and helpful to your patients; however, before you gain that experience and confidence, you should be aware of the many issues that can interfere and make the pilot or co-pilot either want to abort the mission or unwittingly crash the plane. This book covers those potential hazards. More than that, this material is designed to help you arrive at possible destinations.

I chose the title *Beginnings in Psychotherapy* not only to signify that the book is written for people beginning to learn psychotherapy, but also because we'll be making use of many beginning concepts in order to teach technical and theoretical precepts of treatment. We'll address other beginnings—the beginning of a session, for example—as well as derive a beginning understanding of certain basics that apply at both the onset of treatment and throughout its course.

As we address what to do with an initial session, this book provides possible ideas about how to conduct that first session and the early sessions that follow. This book attempts to help both therapist and patient enter psychotherapy through a beginning understanding of what psychotherapy is. Certain complex concepts will be only briefly introduced, because further study of them is beyond the scope of this book.

For those of us who have gone on to become psychoanalysts, we had our own professional beginnings in our early training by first learning about psychotherapy. When I began to learn to do psychotherapy as a medical student and early resident, I recall wanting some kind of a "cookbook" to help me begin. There is no such thing. But that doesn't mean that a concise guide to basic technical and theoretical precepts, applicable to working with all kinds of people with all kinds of problems, isn't possible. These beginning concepts will be introduced in italics.

If we start with the notion that *the first rule is be a human being—after that there are no rules*, what follows are not rules. They are guidelines in helping to navigate the rich, creative, exciting, and confusing field of practicing psychotherapy. This book is designed to help you begin this process of psychotherapy, a process that provides enormous help and satisfaction to your patients and yourself. One of the fundamental pleasures in our field is the pursuit of truth. Because of this goal our field will always endure.

CHAPTER TWO

On meaning—understanding why we do what we do

To practice psychotherapy, you need to understand *why* we do the things we do. Otherwise, you will be following rote instructions that seem arbitrary and odd, and can even interfere with the help you're trying to provide. Let's start from moment one and session one and examine the issue of *meaning* and, specifically, *unconscious meaning*, in the context of what is being said and done in the first clinical interaction.

Imagine yourself about to see a patient for the first time. You're inside an office when the patient arrives outside the office door. To illustrate the importance of meaning, both conscious and unconscious, let's start with something as seemingly meaningless as the position of the door.

Let's consider the position of the door in three possible placements: first, wide open; second, somewhat ajar; and third, closed. One of the first things you're asked to do as a therapist is to notice that something as simple as the placement of the door holds conscious and unconscious meaning that will reflect certain feelings and implications for both you and the patient. Interestingly, during therapy much meaningful interaction takes place without words, as in this example.

A wide open door would seem to mean that you are inviting the patient to enter. I say "seem" since different therapists and patients might glean different meanings from each of these door placements. For some, the wide open door is perhaps a way of saying, "The door is open. I welcome you to walk in." The third position, the door closed, seems to mean that you are setting a boundary: "Do not come in. I'm not available to you."

A door set ajar seems to signal ambivalence on the therapist's part toward the beginning of the session, i.e., "I'm not sure I want you to come in. I may or may not and, therefore, I will position the door so that it is partly closed and partly open." Some of my more honest supervisees have told me that they do this consciously to indicate that they'd like a colleague to enter, but are not yet ready to start a session with a patient.

Why are we concerned with something as trivial as the door's position? It illustrates the sense and meaning that can be derived from one of the most seemingly innocuous parts of early interactions between patient and therapist, and to illustrate the unspoken, and perhaps unconscious, aspects of decisions made by the therapist. I encourage you to think "beyond the door," and notice other things that you do and say in early interactions with patients, looking for their easily missed meaning. What are you communicating by your actions and decisions? What would you like to communicate? I'll be offering other examples shortly.

In addition to looking at the unconscious meaning of your communications, it's important to look at the unconscious meanings of what patients are saying and doing. *Learning to work with the unconscious is a key ingredient in becoming an effective therapist.*

The unconscious is that part of the mind that we're literally not aware of, or not conscious of. Sigmund Freud described the unconscious over a century ago and, despite controversy regarding his work, the unconscious has become a household word and something most people in our culture are aware of, at least to some extent. The unconscious shows itself in dreams, slips, symptoms, and the subtleties of behavior that we're considering here in both patient and therapist. The unconscious has tremendous relevance in our work as therapists, because it holds keys to what is going on behind a patient's conscious thoughts and behaviors. Working with the unconscious provides a multitude of clues about the pain and problems that have brought your patient to you.

The unconscious reveals itself in a myriad of ways in normal everyday life, as well as in the symptoms and problems from which people suffer. I'll provide an obvious example. A college student has an 8:00 a.m. class that she hates. The professor drones on. There's too much work. The student lacks interest in the subject and hates getting up for it. On occasion she forgets to set her alarm to wake up for the class. Although there may be other meanings to her forgetfulness, one of the obvious unconscious meanings of the slip is that she doesn't want to go to this class, and *unconsciously* forgets to set the alarm. You don't have to be Sigmund Freud to recognize that things as simple yet meaningful as this mistake occur all the time in everyday life.

One of the most important steps in becoming a skilled therapist is learning about one's own unconscious. The importance of one's own psychotherapy or analysis cannot be underscored enough; it is a critical part of the process of becoming a therapist. Treatment provides relief from one's own personal symptoms and problems and, importantly, the more we learn about ourselves, the more we can help others learn about themselves. This self-knowledge includes learning about our unconscious. We'll be continuing to look at the unconscious choices that patients and therapists make in the next chapter.

CHAPTER THREE

On gratification and deprivation

"To be a good therapist you need the reins in one hand and a lump of sugar in the other."
—Elvin Semrad (Rako & Mazer, 1980, p. 112)

Another type of beginning moment in the interaction between patient and therapist, perhaps in a clinic or hospital, might be one where the therapist has the option of walking down to a waiting area where patients wait to be escorted by the therapist back to the office. Such a scenario is in contrast to one in which a therapist begins a session by saying to a patient, "I will open my office door on Tuesdays at 4:00 p.m., and that's how you will know we're ready to begin." Some of the differences in these two modes of beginning illustrate important principles that are vital for beginning therapists to understand, including *gratification* and *deprivation*.

The therapist who walks down the hall, greets a patient in the waiting room, and accompanies the patient back is being far more gratifying. He's being "nicer" and more "giving" to the patient. The therapist who is saying that he'll open his door on Tuesdays at 4:00 p.m. is being less gratifying and somewhat more depriving. Is one better and one worse? How do you decide?

These decisions need to be dealt with from the beginning to the end of a treatment, since issues of gratification and deprivation need to be considered throughout a treatment's course. Your decisions may change based on further understanding of these issues. While the therapist who is leaving his door open and not walking down the hall to meet the patient is being less gratifying, on the other hand he may be treating the patient in a more mature, or adult, way. Is the therapist who walks down the hall to greet a patient being too infantilizing toward that person? A goal of any and all therapies is autonomy; if we're doing things that interfere with autonomy and cause excessive dependence, isn't there a serious problem associated with that? One would think so. On the other hand, gratification and deprivation have to be balanced, and should be weighed and provided as needed throughout the course of treatment.

Another example of gratification and deprivation comes from my own practice, in which I saw a patient who told me her former therapist had said to her, "I want you to know I'm there for you. I want you to feel free to call me whenever you feel the need, and if you need to see me, I'll be there for you. I'll make time."

In her offer this therapist was being unusually gratifying. The patient took her up on it. She called her on a Saturday evening, but couldn't reach her by phone. Undaunted, she traveled to the therapist's house, where her office was located. She arrived at the therapist's house as the therapist was about to leave on a date. The therapist explained to the patient that she could not see her then.

This cartoonish vignette reveals much about potential foibles and conflicts that can take place between therapist and patient, leading to these words of advice: *Don't promise more than you can deliver, and don't make threats that you can't, or won't, follow through on.* Elvin Semrad (Rako & Mazer, 1980)

One of the problems of gratification is that too much gratification can turn out to be a seduction and a lie, causing patients to feel disappointed, let down, and lied to. On the other hand, therapists can't simply be depriving and not gratifying at all. A therapist needs to find the delicate balance between gratification and deprivation.

Shortly after my residency I worked in an agency that specialized in the treatment of patients who had problems with alcohol. I found myself supervising a therapist who asked me to help her with her treatment of patients in helping them to control their drinking and other behaviors. She found herself floundering, unable to help many of them. This therapist was a somewhat overweight woman who kept a bowl of candy near her chair, and another bowl by the patient's chair. One of the unconscious meanings of the setting seemed to be the message, "I know *I* can't restrain myself from putting things into my mouth; I assume *you* can't control yourself from putting something in your mouth, either."

As I worked with her in supervision, it became clear that this message may have been contributing to some of the problems she was experiencing with her patients and their issues with putting things in their mouths, including alcohol.

Another example of balancing gratification and deprivation

Early on in my practice, I worked with an angry, young, borderline woman who seemed extremely stormy in our early sessions. She railed loudly against me and became extremely angry in ways that were somewhat frightening for me. At the same time, however, I found the work with her intriguing. As time went on and I tried to work with her despite my own trepidation, her anger seemed to melt away, being replaced by strong dependent yearnings towards me, including the wish to be held when she felt particular emotional pain. In fact, she asked me literally to hold her and hug her in certain sessions. As we talked about this wish, one of the things that I said to her after a while was, "Even if I were to do that, at some point I would have to take away my arms." I wanted her to realize that, after a while, a therapist can't continue to provide gratification. It becomes impossible—a seduction and a lie.

As I mentioned above, one of the goals of treatment is to achieve autonomy and independence. An excessive amount of gratification interferes with such development, produces dependence, counters growing independence, and can interfere with the growth and progress that people need to make in their lives.

For a therapist, one of the most important principles in this balancing act is *giving people what they need*. At times, what someone needs is not necessarily what they ask for, or think they want—and, of course, people need different things at different times. Someone may need limits at one moment, comforting words at another, and silence at the next. As you begin as a therapist, empathy will offer a good orientation point from which to find guidance. We'll be discussing that topic in Section III. In addition, you should work with a supervisor and discuss such issues with him or her. Over time, your experience will help you develop a keener sense of how to balance gratification and deprivation.

SECTION II

TOOLS AND TECHNIQUES

CHAPTER FOUR

On regression and its use

What is regression? Regression is a return to an earlier mode of functioning—for example, a return to thoughts, feelings, and fantasies from childhood. It is also an especially useful element in the process of analytic psychotherapy for *understanding the unconscious*. What that means is that during the course of analytic psychotherapy we want to help the people we're working with to regress in a way that will allow both of us to experience thoughts, feelings, and fantasies that they've encountered at earlier times, which could shed light on symptoms and character troubles that they are having now. We're trying to provide them with a situation that allows them to regress safely, comfortably, and in a controlled way, enabling more access to those thoughts, feelings, and fantasies from the past. This regression allows a systematic exploration of their unconscious, which helps provide new, mature solutions to old, internal, intrapsychic conflict.

We accomplish this through a number of different techniques. These techniques help patients come to terms with—and master—their pain, symptoms, and character problems by accessing parts of their own background and the part of their mind having to do with childhood, namely, their unconscious.

What *techniques* make up the professional methodology we use in order to provide that access? These techniques may seem strange or even bizarre to the beginning therapist—and to patients, as well—because they are quite different from the normal interactions of people in typical contact with friends, colleagues, family members, and others. In fact, it will be helpful to educate patients about why we're doing some of the strange things we do, and to let them know that we're doing them for a purpose. I let patients know that I'm using particular techniques for the benefit of the treatment—for *their* benefit. We'll talk about this issue later on.

Let's review some of those aspects of analytic technique we use to help people achieve the kind of regression needed for us to gain access to the unconscious. One analytic technique is called *abstinence*. Briefly, abstinence means abstaining from providing too many gratifications to a patient. For example, I may *abstain* from providing advice about all kinds of things. Abstinence must be handled in relative terms. Certain types of gratification will need to be provided, and are inevitably provided, during the course of any treatment, whether in psychotherapy or analysis. As I highlight throughout this text, the balance between gratification and deprivation, as well as the role of abstinence, must be weighed sensitively and humanely by each therapist throughout the course of a treatment.

The techniques I'm reviewing have a certain amount of overlap, as is illustrated by an example of the next technique, *anonymity*.

A new patient may ask her new therapist about her religion and whether she's married. The abstinent therapist might not reply, or might reply, "It's better if I don't answer you for the benefit of the treatment." Or the therapist might say, "If you need to know, I'll tell you [if she's really willing to], but if you can tolerate not knowing, that would be better."

All of these procedures are relative in application; they may be modified by your sense of what a person can tolerate. In this last example, the therapist's response provides a certain amount of *abstinence*, i.e., not directly gratifying the patient's wish to learn these personal details about the therapist. The therapist is also being relatively *anonymous* in her response. Additionally, she's being relatively depriving in not declaring the answers immediately.

Early on in treatment, I find it useful to educate patients, especially new and unsophisticated patients, about why I'm doing such things. For example, I might say, "I could answer you, but if I did, it could interfere with our gaining access to thoughts, feelings, and fantasies about me that can be extremely helpful in our work."

Insight-oriented versus supportive approach

I'll give a further clinical example which illustrates other dimensions and benefits of these techniques. Let's say a patient is having trouble asserting herself with her boss and doesn't know what to say to him. A therapist might be tempted to provide certain suggestions, offer advice, or even supply direct quotations to a patient, actually providing a script of what to say to the boss. Some patients need this kind of direction. Many people, however, do not need such structured guidance, and would benefit more by having their inhibition in assertiveness explored. What is the patient anxious about? Is there a particular fantasy (perhaps unconscious) of what might happen if she spoke up assertively? Providing direct advice could actually *deprive* a patient of the opportunity to learn more about themselves and their unconscious, an opportunity to become far better equipped to master new situations involving assertiveness than just possessing a situation-specific "answer." Using our example, the answer to what a patient should do with her boss begins to become more comprehensible to her as she understands more about herself. And she learns about herself through her therapy using the techniques we're discussing, which allow a regression to take place. Thus our examination of these issues highlights one of the differences between "insight-oriented" and "supportive" psychotherapy.

Transference

Anonymity is only relative. Patients will learn things about us, whether from our type of dress, the office in which we practice, the language we use, or any of an infinite number of other ways. Still, anonymity matters in therapy.

One reason for fostering relative anonymity is that we don't want to interfere with the development of thoughts, feelings, or fantasies about *us*, a phenomenon called *transference*. Transference develops in the regressive crucible of the treatment and has unique therapeutic value. It involves the displacement of thoughts, feelings, and fantasies, originally about important figures in childhood, onto the therapist. Although the phenomenon of transference is more pronounced and available in psychoanalysis, transference derivatives frequently occur in analytic psychotherapy. I find that understanding and interpreting transference can also be quite important to the process of psychoanalytic psychotherapy. Therefore, one of our techniques is to avoid interfering with such an important regressive phenomenon—for example, by not providing too much reality about ourselves as therapists. Transference provides vital and helpful clues about the past, and about why patients are feeling what they're feeling about others outside the treatment. The therapy relationship repeats and replays this and starts to come alive and flourish through the development of transference. This process can actually be interfered with, and stifled by, giving too much information about oneself.

These phenomena speak towards another interesting and paradoxical part of the therapeutic process. Normally in friendship there is a give-and-take about the personal details of both people. If we are being too much of a "friend" and providing too much reality to the people that we're working with, we can paradoxically end up taking away therapeutic opportunities and helping people less.

Countertransference: Regression in the therapist

Regression in psychotherapy is not confined to the patient. *Countertransference* involves a fascinating regression on the part of the therapist. As we sit, listen, and intervene, part of the creative pleasure in doing this kind of work involves paying attention to what we're thinking, feeling, and fantasizing about. It's been said everything that occurs within us as we sit with patients has something to do with the patient. Although I haven't always found that to be the case, what I'm thinking and feeling is often a source of surprising and relevant insight about the patient. Of course, that doesn't mean that we're sharing all of these thoughts and feelings with the patient, but we're paying attention to it as a valuable source of understanding. Countertransference is an enjoyable, creative, and helpful part of the work we do. Because of its major importance, you will find examples of countertransference throughout this book.

Countertransference involves a phenomenon similar to transference, this time occurring on the part of the therapist toward the patient. Thoughts, feelings, and fantasies from the therapist may be displaced onto the patient as part of the regression that can take place within the therapist in the analytic situation. At times, the term "countertransference" is used more generically to refer to any reaction that a therapist is having toward his patient. Sometimes it's also defined as a "reaction" on the part of the therapist "to the patient's transference" (Moore & Fine, 1990, p. 47).

Importantly, these reactions within a therapist provide valuable clues and insights about the patient and about the therapeutic interaction between the two participants. In addition, the analytic therapeutic atmosphere can reveal much to the therapist about himself as these regressive phenomena continue in both participants.

Neutrality

The next technique we'll discuss that is used in the promotion of a therapeutic regression is our use of *neutrality*. Neutrality was defined by Anna Freud as the analyst "being equidistant between id, ego, and superego" (Moore & Fine, 1990, p. 127).

Neutrality implies positioning oneself neither on the side of patients giving in to urges nor on the side of moralizing. It involves avoiding the imposition of values on the patient. Another implication of neutrality is "avoiding extremes of involvement, i.e., extremes of detachment and over involvement" (Moore & Fine, 1990, p. 127). In general, I find myself trying to be a "helpful ally" (Freud 1940, as cited in Moore & Fine, 1990, p. 127).

Neutrality implies, among other things, that the therapist is *not being judgmental*. By avoiding a judgmental stance, a therapist helps to create an atmosphere of freedom, a critical dimension of the therapy. We want the individuals we're working with to be as free as possible to talk about anything and everything that crosses their minds. Anything that inhibits this freedom to talk is an interference.

I'll give an obvious, cartoonish example of such interference. A patient comes in to his therapist and the patient says, "Doctor, I had a homosexual dream about you last night."

The doctor responds by saying, "That's disgusting!"

You can imagine the inhibition in freedom resulting from the outrageous interjection of that homophobic therapist.

A less cartoonish example: A married man, a health professional, who is in his mid-thirties and has been having serious marital troubles, presents for treatment. He's been chronically unhappy for many years with his wife, and sees her as rigid and preventing him from having fun. He finds himself falling in love with somebody he works with, and begins to think about having an affair with this person. He asks the therapist, "Should I do it or not? Should I have the affair, or should I not?"

I suppose a non-neutral, advice-giving therapist could give two different types of advice. One type of non-neutral advice would be from the Sixties-influenced "if it feels good do it" type of therapist (that is, a therapist of the id). This therapist could say, "Sure, go for it. You only live once."

The other type of advice that a therapist could give would be moralistic—on the side of the superego. This superego therapist could say, "Of course not. You're a married man. That would be a horrible thing to do!"

Through these examples, one can see that a therapist's bias can interfere with the *freedom* of the people that he's working with. A judgmental attitude can interfere with the patients' comfort, as well as their willingness to bring all kinds of honest thoughts and feelings to the treatment. In the case of the patient considering an affair, even though a therapist might internally feel critical when hearing about such a problem, he or she should be aware that coming across as critical will likely inhibit the person from being able to spontaneously, freely, thoroughly, and analytically discuss and analyse the problem he's having. If our behavior is something other than neutral, we threaten to inhibit and restrict the analytic process, the process of understanding.

Safety and freedom

As therapists, we're trying to provide an atmosphere of safety as thoroughly and consistently as possible throughout the course of the treatment. One of the reasons for this concern for safety is the need for another element of the treatment situation to be present if it is to succeed and flourish: the therapeutic situation must *allow a sense of freedom.*

A patient needs to know he's free to speak about anything and everything. This sense of security requires an atmosphere of freedom from criticism, retaliation, seduction, and anything else that can restrict one's sense of safety. An atmosphere of safety is part of the context that allows a treatment to take place—a context that provides the kind of relief from pain that we, as therapists, hope to provide.

An atmosphere of safety is necessary in order for a regression to take place and for both participants to succeed in their therapeutic endeavor. As you can see, the element of safety overlaps with many other issues discussed in this guide.

Confidentiality

Another aspect of the therapeutic setting that facilitates regression is confidentiality. Once again, confidentiality is of utmost importance in being able to provide an atmosphere where patients feel *safe and free* from harm. One way people feel harmed is through the betrayal of the intimate thoughts, feelings, and fantasies discussed in a psychotherapy session. The assurance and awareness of confidentiality allows people to talk about potentially embarrassing or painful thoughts, feelings, and fantasies that are typically restricted in discussion.

As with every technique and procedure that we're discussing, reality and circumstances can make confidentiality a relative term. For example, hospitals, clinics, and even legal requirements in private practice typically require record keeping and charting which impact and interfere with confidentiality. However, as best as possible, confidentiality needs to be preserved to ensure the sense of safety so critical to the developing process.

The need for confidentiality should also be followed by supervisors and in classroom settings. The style with which students report the details of a psychotherapy session obviously has implications regarding confidentiality. Let's consider the differences between students in supervision who tape record sessions, take notes during a session, or take notes after a session is over.

How might a person feel who has agreed to be tape recorded by his therapist? Obviously, there can be a host of reactions, including questions asked or unspoken, such as, "How will this recording be used? Who will be listening to it?" Unconscious or conscious urges to inhibit material may arise in both therapist and patient, which can skew—and interfere with—the analytic process. Conversely, exhibitionistic urges may become stimulated in both patient and therapist. These two potential problems are only two of the issues that could arise from tape-recording sessions.

Could similar issues arise with note taking during a session? Of course. A patient might think, "Is my therapist more interested in the notes than in me?" "Who is he sharing these notes with?" "I wish he were more with me and less with the writing." These thoughts may go unspoken by both parties until they're brought overtly into the process.

In general, writing notes following a session tends to be less intrusive and disruptive as a technique for students. Nevertheless, patients in clinics and training programs may need to become aware that their therapist is in training, leading to fantasies about supervisors as well as who else is privy to their material. When and how the confidentiality issues presented by training should be dealt with is a sensitive and important issue for beginning students to discuss, and frequently arises in both supervision and in the treatment.

Time: Frequency and timelessness

Another technique used in allowing a therapeutic regression to take place involves the frequency of sessions. As an exaggerated example, imagine the difference between a patient who comes five times a week and a patient who comes once a year for a session. For the person who comes once a year, inevitably the most superficial, "current events-like" material is all that would likely come up: "It's been a good year. This is what happened at work; this is what happened with my spouse. Nice to see you. See you again next year."

When a patient comes in several times a week, regression is furthered, which provides the sense that one can *confide* and reveal more with increased opportunity. Increased frequency of sessions also produces a greater sense of temptation, in that transference yearnings are mobilized towards the therapist as session frequency increases. In addition to allowing more regressive material to come to the forefront, the sense of continuity created by a more frequent treatment enhances a therapist's ability to understand more about the patient. In addition, with more sessions, more work can be done.

Typically, in analytic psychotherapy, there is no deadline for the end of treatment. The sense of timelessness that this engenders also furthers the regression and enhances the treatment.

Free association

Another element of the therapeutic setting that facilitates regression is *free association*, when we ask patients to say out loud whatever crosses their minds. This is no easy task, since people are used to censoring a host of thoughts and feelings in normal interaction. The motivation to censor comes from inhibition about too much intimate exposure of themselves. However, such exposure is precisely what we need as a therapeutic team to gain as much access as possible to their unconscious.

People worry that they might embarrass themselves by saying things that convey sexual and aggressive impulses that they want to keep hidden. Fear of humiliation is only one resistance to free association; multiple sources of inhibiting influences produce a strong wish to censor.

Conscious and unconscious fears about what patients will learn about themselves, and also reveal to a therapist, are universal. When you ask a patient to say everything, you are also, in effect, requesting them to allow themselves to regress. Free association allows thoughts, feelings, and fantasies from the past to be exposed—and, as with all of the other techniques we're discussing, provides helpful entry to their unconscious (the regressive part of the mind). Free association leads to new and different associations, as well as expanding access to more and more unconscious material.

Although asking patients to say everything that goes through their minds is the fundamental rule of psychoanalysis, I find that I do not limit this technique to patients in psychoanalysis. I also do this with psychotherapy patients who I think can work in an analytic and insight-oriented way. The use of free association, in and of itself, produces a regression in that we're asking that there be no holds barred on anything and everything—including those kinds of regressive phenomena that take place in the mind—in a way that we don't normally allow in normal conversation or typical relationships outside of a treatment.

Silence

Silence is yet another procedure that we use to promote regression. The judicious use of silence helps the people we're working with to make more unconscious contact with what they're thinking, as well as feel their feelings. Then, as a result of the silence, they can further access and say what they're thinking and feeling. A therapist's silence, and the regression it fosters, can place in bold relief the thoughts, feelings, and fantasies taking place in a patient's mind, when we don't distract them with our own comments. Ultimately, silence on the part of the therapist furthers their understanding of their unconscious and, ultimately, why they're thinking and feeling these things.

With one woman with whom I worked early on in my practice, I found that all I had to do was wait and be silent at the beginning of the session and, within a short time, she would burst into tears and begin feeling some of the pain that had brought her to me.

Ambiguity

One result of what we're doing in the analytic situation is creating *ambiguity*. Patients are not exactly sure what will arise in them. They're uncertain about what we, as therapists, are thinking or feeling, as well. They're also not exactly sure what may happen in this situation. In addition to asking them to say everything that they're thinking and feeling, we don't give specific instructions.

One of the consequences of the regression includes the transferential reactions that we've begun to discuss. Transference derivatives frequently appear during the course of analytic psychotherapy. The development of transference reactions, their elucidation, and their connections to the past and present are part of the work of psychotherapy. These transferential reactions can be confusing amidst the ambiguity of the analytic situation.

A woman I worked with years ago came to treatment, in part, due to serious concerns that she experienced with her marriage. She felt she no longer loved her husband, grew interested in other men, and felt bewildered by these feelings. As the treatment progressed, she felt comforted by having me to talk with. She felt understood and safe, and told me she looked forward to seeing me. It also became clear to me that she was beginning to feel affectionately towards me. She began to talk of enjoying the "secretiveness of our relationship." She spoke of how close she felt to me, and of her awareness that she thought about me between sessions. At the end of a particular session, she stood up and looked as if she wanted to hug me as she took a step toward me and opened her arms. When she did this, I stood relatively still.

At the next session I told her, "It seemed to me that you looked like you wanted to hug me." She acknowledged it, and we talked about it at length, picking up on the many things connected to this desire. I let her know that if we understood all of her impulses and feelings in words, instead of actions, she would find it far more helpful than acting on her impulses, even if she also felt frustrated or disappointed by not acting. Though frustrated, she tolerated her frustration. I explained that this preserved me as a therapist, which was my role and what she needed me for. I could do far more for her as a therapist than as a lover, no matter how powerful the upsurge of these affectionate and erotic feelings might be.

In fact, my letting her know that this was a place where she was safe from a return seduction allowed her to learn more about the historical roots of the problem she was experiencing with her husband, as well as the roots of the erotic transference that appeared in the treatment.

She initially found her erotic transferential reaction confusing, and the ambiguity of the situation further confused her (i.e., could this be a place where affectionate or sexual feelings could actually be acted on?). Ultimately, however, the treatment, which allowed those feelings to develop, proved useful in elucidating various elements of her symptoms in her outside life and the past in terms of an erotized relationship with her father and an older brother. Over time, as her understanding of herself grew, the work in the treatment helped her marriage improve. She and her husband changed in interesting and complementary ways that provided more intimacy for both of them. She became less interested in the "forbidden man" inside and outside the treatment, and was more fully able to direct sexual and affectionate wishes to the man who was available to her—her husband. The patient and the marriage both improved.

When patients know that they won't be seduced or retaliated against as aggressive and sexual urges emerge in a treatment, they can feel safe and can progress in their treatment. The ambiguity of not knowing exactly what will happen in a treatment adds to the regression, as a treatment takes its inevitable twists and turns. That ambiguity is yet another element of this fascinating and complex setting in which we allow ourselves to work.

The couch

Another technique that is not used in psychotherapy but is used in psychoanalysis to encourage regression is the *use of the couch*. The use of the couch puts the analyst out of visual contact with the patient. This is a kind of regressogenic technique that allows for less reality to impinge so that more regressive phenomena can occur. The element of stimulus deprivation helps produce this therapeutic regression. Even though the couch is not used in analytic psychotherapy, I mention it to further a student's understanding of other techniques that are used to promote regression in other therapeutic settings, like psychoanalysis.

CHAPTER FIVE

The frame

> *Your love never changes*
> *It's like a picture in a frame, and it remains the same.*
>
> —Anita Baker, recording artist*
> (see lyric acknowledgment)

What is the frame in psychotherapy? The frame is a metaphor that captures certain important aspects of the treatment situation. Jose Bleger defined it as representing "the constants within whose limits the process occurs" (Langs, 1981, p. 466). It's also been referred to as a kind of "bulwark" (Baranger, W. & Baranger, M., 1961–2), (Langs, 1981, p. 466). The analytic situation provides a "stable *frame* of reference within which the patient and therapist, or analyst, mobilize in each other intra-psychic processes that help the patient work towards movement, insight, and change" (Moore & Fine, 1990, p. 15).

Briefly described, the analytic therapeutic situation takes place in a particular setting at a *consistent time and frequency* that also provides other constants. Once again, all of this consistency is meant to establish the analytic therapeutic situation, in which the unconscious is elucidated and explored for therapeutic purposes. The primary aim is to help the patient achieve increasingly mature conscious solutions to his problems.

The frame represents the constancy of the treatment, which in and of itself provides the properties of a "container" (Bion, 1962, p. 91), (Moore & Fine, 1990, p. 32), or, as Winnicott (Winnicott, 1969, pp. 711–716) referred to it, a "holding environment." Certain elements are common to all of the metaphors and descriptions that have been used: constancy, consistency, limits, and boundaries (Moore & Fine, 1990). Let's talk about all of them.

Time

Time is one of the elements of the frame. Typically a treatment begins at a certain time and ends at a certain time. I use 45 minutes as the amount of time provided for a session, although in the past it was most common for therapists to allot 50 minutes to each session. Imagine, if you would, a variation in the time frame in which a therapist used 45 minutes at certain sessions, and at other sessions switched to 50 or 55 minutes. What might a patient think when the therapist returned to the use of a 45-minute session? Perhaps, "You don't like me as much as you did last time. Now I'm boring you?"

Constancy and consistency are an important part of what the frame provides. The amount of time is simply one piece of the frame, however. A person might feel somewhat differently jostled if you moved their appointment to a different day or time—for example, from Tuesday at 5:00 p.m. to Thursday at 8:00 a.m. They would experience a certain feeling of being jockeyed and, perhaps, uncertainty in connection with switching. "What's next?" they might wonder.

Conversely and paradoxically, treatment possesses an element of timelessness, as we've discussed. Typically the length of time in which a treatment will transpire has no fixed deadline. Time limits for the treatment as a whole are suspended. One element of the unconscious is also a kind of timelessness, in which kaleidoscopic changes from past to present (and vice versa) occur routinely.

The physical office

Another part of the frame is the actual office setting in which the treatment takes place. Therapists' offices vary greatly, depending on the amount of space a therapist has available, the room's location (in a private office, clinic, or hospital), and whether the room itself changes due to administrative constraints.

Some therapists may prefer to be physically closer to those they work with than others, for both conscious and unconscious reasons. The physical distance between patient and therapist can be meaningful. One can imagine a patient's reaction to a therapist who moves his chair closer to, or further away from, the patient at different sessions. Such inconsistency would undoubtedly evoke multiple reactions in patients who come to rely upon those aspects of physical consistency that exist in the framework of a treatment.

A young woman with whom I worked had been sexually abused by an older brother. The violation of her physical boundaries made her keenly sensitive to any change in the distance between our chairs. She had remained vigilantly on alert ever since her abuse experience.

This need for environmental consistency need not mean that a robotic sameness is necessary. Changes of frame occur in all kinds of ways over time, whether due to a therapist's move to a different office (a not infrequent event during the career of a therapist), or to more minor shifts in the physical environment.

For example, a clock I had used in my office for some years broke and couldn't be repaired. While looking for a replacement, I found two, both of which I thought might be suitable, but wanted to see how they'd do in my office. I wanted to ensure that I would be able to see the new clock easily, without needlessly and tactlessly staring at it during sessions. I decided to give each of them a "try-out" for a day.

Although most patients didn't consciously notice the change, one person definitely did. In fact, she became frightened by it.

Maria was a 30-year-old borderline woman with whom I'd worked for several years. She was one of multiple siblings from a wealthy family whose father often travelled for business. Her cold, unempathic mother left the children's caretaking to a large staff of nannies, cooks, and housekeepers, whom she frequently fired. The empathic laxity in Maria's upbringing, as well as other problems, led to a great sense of internal fragility and an outbreak of a number of symptoms once the patient reached adolescence.

During the patient's childhood and adolescence, her mother, an extremely narcissistic woman, went through a period of heavy drinking where she took to her bedroom for prolonged periods of time during the day.

The family was a very religious one. At one point, various religious figures—priests, bishops, and even cardinals—visited frequently. There were subtle encouragements for having "religious experiences." These included episodes of altered states of consciousness in which the patient saw visions of Jesus or the Virgin Mary. Her family excitedly discussed and encouraged these episodes. This pressure seems to have interfered with Maria's reality testing and sense of self. Additionally, the patient witnessed the visiting religious figures "talking in tongues," which the patient described as odd utterances while they were in an altered state of consciousness. She found this frightening and confusing. This particular patient came to rely on my regularity, consistency, and sameness, using these traits to identify with, incorporate, regulate, and produce a steadier sense of self. In addition to feeling steadied and supported by my general personal qualities and demeanor, she also felt safe through the sameness of the frame, including my physical office. Her seeing my use of two different clocks in a short period of time frightened her, and made her feel during one session that something was wrong with me—maybe I had "gone crazy"—something she feared in her mother and in herself.

We talked about and interpreted this poignant and relatively short-lived treatment phenomenon, leading to an interesting piece of therapeutic work. It also highlighted for me how a seemingly minor change in the frame of the physical setting can produce important effects. It helped me to attend to other such changes, listening for derivatives of them in patient material.

Not all patients will respond to these kinds of frame changes. The frame will have varying degrees of importance for different patients. At times, I've thought I could work with or analyse certain patients anywhere, because they are so impervious to changes in the frame. I have, however, noticed that some deviations in the frame, such as interruptions in the treatment, frequently tend to elicit reactions from patients.

The unconscious, in all its primitivity, does not work via the golden rule, "Do unto others as you'd have them do unto you." Instead it functions in a much more primitive manner using Talion Law, exemplified by Hammurabi's Code and its declaration of *an eye for an eye, a tooth for a tooth.* Thus, a missed session on a therapist's part may evoke a reaction in kind by a patient, who may slip and forget a session or arrive late to a session or sessions. Sometimes a patient may merely associate to their own departure as a more subtle expression of this reaction.

Money

Arrangements about money form another part of the frame. Some therapists prefer to be paid each session, others once a month. Conscious and unconscious factors determine how a therapist arranges payment, as do factors imposed on therapists who work in clinics with their own unique set of rules. However, I encourage beginning therapists to consider unconscious meanings and implications in making choices with how they work with money. Seemingly irrelevant or trivial parts of the frame may have more meaning than first meets the eye.

I knew of a senior analyst who told his patients they must always pay at the same session he gave them their bill. To me this has a graspy, greedy feeling to it which undoubtedly could have been picked up by his patients.

Some therapists find they have trouble being paid on time. Beginning therapists should consider such matters carefully, paying attention to how their own countertransference issues and problems may impinge on the way they handle this frame issue. The best way to handle money owed by patients is not to let this problem develop to begin with. You can't be a therapist and a lender at the same time.

Are there problems associated with a patient who asks you if they can pay with cash? I believe there are. The patient may have a fantasy that the therapist is not declaring the cash as income. The problems with this situation are obvious. If the patient is led to question a therapist's honesty, then doesn't that make the whole treatment situation seem a sham? It would seem so.

Handling missed sessions

In his early writings, Freud advocated that analysts charge patients for missed sessions. We'll consider this frame issue here. There are two main reasons for charging patients for missed sessions. One is clinical, the other practical. Freud indicated that, since resistance (which we'll discuss later) is universal, it will inevitably appear in all kinds of manifestations, including missed sessions. He indicated that the frequency of missed sessions decreases with a policy where patients are responsible for their time, whether they use it or not.

It would be hypocritical to leave out the other reason for such a policy: namely, a practical one. The treatment is also how we earn our livelihood. We have only so many hours per week. Too many missed sessions create serious adverse financial effects. A policy of patient responsibility, on the other hand, treats a session time analogously to the rental of an apartment. A tenant pays for the rental of the apartment (rental of the time) whether it's used or not.

I advocate such a policy for both clinical and practical reasons, and use it in my own practice. When I explain my policy to patients, I tell them that if I can fill their time, or if they can make it up, they're not responsible for both the original time *and* the make-up, as that would constitute double charging. I believe that a certain amount of countertransference anger (using the term more generally) frequently arises without the use of such a payment policy. In those therapists whom I've supervised over the years, I've seen that the reluctance to use this type of policy reflects a countertransference problem involving either an over-identification with the patient or, more commonly, a fear of their patient's anger in response to this policy.

CHAPTER SIX

Creating a therapeutic atmosphere

Other unique aspects of the therapeutic frame are harder to define. These aspects have to do with the therapist's basic attitude and demeanor. They involve a particular emotional and affective climate, or atmosphere, established in a treatment. Therapists vary in their capacity for warmth, empathy, friendliness, calmness, objectivity, limit setting, etc. It is my belief that establishing an ongoing atmosphere of consistency, empathy, warmth, and calm is extremely important in establishing a treatment, and this exists as the therapeutic atmosphere aspect of the treatment's frame.

Early teachers of mine indicated the need for a therapist to be a "blank slate" in order to allow for a regression to take place and to serve as a screen upon which patients could project transferences. Although neutrality and relative blankness are useful, they need to be balanced by the need for humanity. We're trying to establish, above all, an atmosphere of *safety* where all is allowed to be said. Unending stony blankness by itself might have the opposite effect.

Another extreme example of an unsafe atmosphere would be frighteningly different affective moods on the part of the therapist. If a therapist's affect varies too much between, or within, sessions, one can imagine the effect. Similarly, if a therapist is too affectionate or overly involved in a patient's life, this may also seduce, disturb, or frighten a patient. Ultimately our main function is to be a *translator*. Anything else could be a seduction and a lie. More on this later.

A calm demeanor is needed but that also needs to be balanced. Spontaneity is, and should be, part of the repertoire of a therapist, and this spontaneity includes affective reactions. I see it as a caricatured version of a psychoanalyst or a psychotherapist to be a completely blank, unexpressive figure. As you can see it's a delicate balance.

Laughter with a patient (of course not *at* a patient), wincing in response to something painful, and the like—all these should be part of the normal, healthy, flexible, empathic atmosphere that exists in an optimal analytic psychotherapeutic climate. I am not advocating the production of a line of analytic robots, silent except for the occasional grunted "uh huh," a macabre version of a 1950s analyst. Our humanity, flexibility, and spontaneity needs to be part of the climate. Each of us varies in our capacity to provide or withhold. A patient's needs should dictate how and when a therapist shows emotion. These needs vary from person to person and from moment to moment during the course of a treatment.

The therapist has a responsibility to protect patients from intrusions upon privacy and confidentiality. For example, when insurance companies ask for information about a patient, my policy is to give out as little information as possible. These aspects of the frame must also be attended to by every therapist.

The therapist needs to monitor consistently the boundaries that exist between patient and therapist. While a grotesque violation of this can take place—when a disturbed therapist makes use of a patient for sexual purposes, for example—many violations of the frame's boundaries can take place in more subtle ways. For example, a therapist may use a patient for excessive personal gratification or narcissistic gain. These can take forms as varied as a narcissistic therapist regularly giving advice or seer-like pronouncements for his own aggrandizement, or keeping patients in treatment for too long a time for one's own personal financial gain.

The therapeutic alliance

I believe that the sense of safety and freedom are part of the context that leads to what's called *the therapeutic alliance*. The therapeutic alliance helps in moving a treatment forward.

The therapeutic alliance begins to take hold in a treatment as the therapeutic process is initiated. It has been defined differently by different authors. Although transferential reactions are an important part of a treatment, not everything constitutes transference. The process of forming an alliance starts from moment one, day one, and is marked by the beginning of a sense of collaboration and cooperation on the part of both parties. Negative transferential feelings and enactments may interfere with this; however, I believe that this sense of a joint venture, a "we-ness," is necessary for a treatment to work. It is an engagement on the part of a therapist and patient to work together for the common cause of helping the patient. Both parties are motivated in this venture due to that common cause and common goals, including the relief of a patient's pain.

Transferential reactions on the part of the patient, and countertransferential reactions on the therapist's part, can operate at times in every treatment to interfere with or undermine the treatment's progression. Yet I have found that when the going gets tough, as it frequently can, it's the therapeutic alliance that can help in seeing the job through. The term itself gives clues to its meaning: both parties are *allies*. They come together in joint work and collaboration, with a shared interest and motivation to reach the goal of relieving pain, helping a person to become a more comfortable, more mature version of him or herself as a result of the psychotherapeutic work.

At times I've found sessions akin to a "huddle" in football. The teammates get together regularly, meet for a time, and assist each other as teammates getting to the goal. They're on the same side. Indeed, you as a therapist must be allied with your patient if a treatment is to work.

At certain times, you can't be an ally to a prospective patient, or at least you may become a less than optimal one. I'll give some examples. If I'm seeing one spouse, say the wife of a couple, for a time, and the husband wants to see me as well, there's a problem with that rooted in the therapeutic alliance. The husband could accurately see me as his wife's therapist, which would interfere with his alliance with me. It could also interfere with my alliance with the wife, if seeing the husband as a patient seems to pose a potential threat to her confidentiality. In such a case, I would suggest that the husband see someone else.

I know of other situations where the sense of alliance could also be compromised. I knew of a patient in treatment with an analyst in a particular community. The treatment seemed to have various problems, leading the patient to seek an outside consultation with another therapist to see whether another perspective could clarify the problems with the treatment. The outside consultant, once the consultation began, realized that he was a close friend of the patient's therapist. He then informed the patient of that fact and stated that he should not perform the consultation, since their friendship would interfere with his objectivity. Importantly, he added that he needed to be this patient's ally in order to perform the consultation, and pointed out that the friendship between the two therapists would interfere with his taking on that role.

When things become difficult, as is the case in many a treatment, the therapeutic alliance is needed so that both parties can hang in there and work through the infinite number of potential challenges that can arise in a treatment. The therapeutic alliance is, therefore, a necessary and very important part of any treatment. I believe that this type of alliance is furthered by the climate and setting that I've been describing and advocating throughout this text.

Psychotherapy is a cooperative venture that requires mutuality in order for the partners entering it to work and learn together. This venture is influenced by both transferential and nontransferential elements. One of the early tasks of the therapist is to engage a patient in this task and work with the resistances, both conscious and unconscious, that inevitably arise from start to finish.

As the process of discovery continues, and as a patient *feels* you to be on their side, the therapeutic alliance grows. Patient and therapist become allies in this mutual process of discovery that helps to reduce a patient's pain. It's easier for two people to handle pain than one alone. If you take a thorn out of someone's paw, they'll naturally begin to perceive you as an ally—and, as a result, you begin to become one.

CHAPTER SEVEN

The consultation

The initial portion of a treatment, called *the consultation*, is different from what follows. Of course it means what it says; the patient is consulting you about their problems. It's done in the context of everything we've discussed so far. It's done empathically, sensitively, with appreciation of the pain and discomfort someone experiences in revealing intimate information to a stranger, information they may never have discussed with anyone else. It may be particularly hard to share this information with someone they don't know. On the other hand, they may find relief in speaking with someone whom they feel will be objective and separate from their outside life.

Various tasks take place simultaneously in the early consultative sessions of a treatment. As you begin to develop an atmosphere in which a patient feels safe, you start to engage the patient in the process of inquiry.

The initial session frequently starts with an inquiry about why they've contacted you. On a personal note, I start consultations with a piece of history from my own personal beginnings, a detail that comes from my father, a clinical psychologist. Years ago, he mentioned to me that he began sessions by asking, "How can I be of help?" I often begin sessions in this way. There are, of course, innumerable alternative ways of beginning.

If the information isn't spontaneously forthcoming, I ask about recent pain, recent history, and recent symptoms. The answers may unfold naturally and spontaneously, but if not, early on I begin to inquire about people's histories, since without that, I feel as though I'm working in the dark. I try to learn about childhood, important family members, parents, siblings, and so on. This information provides a historical context that allows understanding and insights to develop.

I have found in supervising young M.D.s over the years that I've had to "de-medicalize" them in connection with the work of a therapist. For example, residents have been taught to use a "SCID" interview (Structured Clinical Interview for DSM IV), or others like it, which are formal ways of asking questions and determining symptoms to reach a diagnosis and, frequently, to determine and initiate the use of a medicine. This methodology has its place in the diagnostic evaluation of patients, and in psychopharmacology intervention.

However, I find the use of such an interview process problematic as a means to initiate psychotherapy. It skews the analytic therapeutic process in which we're engaging the patient, and often prevents the patient from being able to go where he or she needs to go. If you follow a checklist agenda, especially for a prolonged amount of time, you may not end up with a psychotherapy patient—more likely you'll end up with a medication management patient. Imagine how the patient would feel when they are immediately confronted by such a systematized, rote inquiry. That kind of approach certainly would not further the sense of connection that supports the therapeutic alliance.

Now I'll state something that may sound thoroughly contrary to what I just expressed above. It's important to gather basic information about your patient in a non-intrusive and non-rigid manner. I've heard presentations from some analysts who have shared the information they gathered in initial sessions where countertransference and other subjective issues so dominated the presentation that I hadn't learned how old the patient was.

I do believe in a certain structure and method of inquiry that should exist at the onset of a treatment. This structure should give way to a more free-form, free-associative process as time goes on. In my residency training, we were asked to do a one-session evaluation that noted the patient's chief complaint, history of recent illness, past and family history, and so on. Personally, I found covering all of this territory in one session rushed, too structured, unempathic, and machine-like. On the other hand, this data is important information we need in order to proceed. I typically now see a patient for multiple sessions, doing a consultation over several visits, before I have a sense of what's going on and what's needed. While we need certain basic information and, without it, are working in the dark, it needs to be elicited empathically, sensitively, and thoroughly.

Understanding the specific recent symptoms and the recent pain a person is experiencing that causes them to call us is crucial, as is understanding the patient's background. If this information doesn't unfold in the course of the opening sessions, at a later time I ask about it, perhaps pointing out the patient's uneasiness about revealing it. The process of inquiry is even more neutral and abstinent when evaluating someone who seems appropriate for analysis rather than psychotherapy.

The analytic inquiry

To reiterate, when initiating a consultation, I do ask in some manner how I can be of help. This question tends to lead to a discussion of what's happening in the patient's life. I investigate what symptoms they've experienced as well as what they think is causing the pain. What's the pain like, and where is it coming from? I try to determine how long the symptoms and pain have been there in their recent onset, and what prompted the call to me. I try to determine the triggers for the pain.

I ask about the current situation. I ask and obtain information about the patient and important figures in his/her life. I ask about marriage, partners, children, and other important life figures, as well as current life details: jobs, school, and the like. Many paths of inquiry are illuminated and determined by the unique details of each patient's history, and which naturally point the way in exploration.

Obtaining a past history is critical, as well. I need to understand what parents were like, including the basics: Are they still alive? What are their personalities like, now and in the past? I ask about siblings and their personalities. The patient's academic history and job history are also revealing. So are friendships, past and present. I'll ask about boyfriends, girlfriends, and whatever sexual issues seem relevant. We want to understand the development of their life as a whole as it progressed over the years. Has there been trauma? Sometimes this information unfolds naturally, and I just sit back and listen. At times, it doesn't, and I may become aware of glaring gaps in my knowledge regarding all kinds of details. At some point I may help a patient observe they haven't mentioned particular areas. You may choose to note out loud that you haven't heard about X, Y, or Z as part of their lives. A patient's silence about something may represent conflict about that particular part of his or her life. Hearing too much about one particular area may represent conflict, as well.

I've found that without understanding presenting complaints, recent history, past history, parents, siblings, childhood, and so on, I'm working blind. I don't have the context I need to understand what's happening or what's being repeated. What patterns are emerging? With whom is the patient identifying? My understanding of the past invariably elucidates and illuminates the present. Another area of inquiry during the consultation is the patient's history of previous treatment. I try to learn about previous therapists and therapy, how long the treatment lasted, and what precipitated the need for these previous treatments. I try to learn about the use of medication currently and previously, as well as other specifics about medications, i.e., dosages and the length of time the patient used them.

Although you'll intuit much just from being in the room with a patient, understanding more of the details of what happened invariably helps. One context for the present is the past and, without knowing about the patient's past, you're at a disadvantage as a therapist in your ability to help.

SECTION III

GUIDEPOSTS FOR OUR WORK IN LISTENING AND INTERVENING

CHAPTER EIGHT

Guideposts for our work in listening and intervening

Empathy

Empathy is the cornerstone of psychotherapy. It is the most fundamental part of what we do as therapists. Empathy guides us through the twists and turns of listening, talking, and understanding. It informs us about what to do, what not to do, when to do it, how to do it, and so on. Empathy is not our only source of guidance and orientation, but it's the single most basic tool for therapists.

So what is it? Empathy is a process. It's the process of trying to understand what it's like to be someone else. Empathy is frequently spoken of as an attempt to feel what the other is feeling, but it goes beyond feeling. It involves trying to understand what it's actually like to *be someone else.*

The empathic process has different parts. It is a mind probe that helps us to understand what it's like to be the other. It helps us understand the pain someone else is in—and, of course, that's critical to understand, since that's what brought our patients to us and what we're trying to help them with. But the empathic process doesn't end there. It also involves putting into words what we understand of what they are thinking, feeling, and fantasizing about.

More technically, empathy involves a trial identification with the other, then a pulling back in order to provide your patient with a sense of what it is that you've understood about them.

Empathy involves dosage, timing, and tact.

Dosage: People need to hear what they can tolerate, but not too much and not too little.

Timing: Empathy also involves the judicious use of timing. What a person is ready to hear and respond to at the beginning of a session may be quite different from what he or she can hear at the end of that same session. What they're ready to hear in session one is different from what they're ready for in session one hundred and one.

Tact: We always keep self-esteem in mind as we talk and listen.

In a way, we're all the same. We have the same feelings, needs, and wishes. Our understanding of ourselves guides our understanding of others. As we put ourselves in our patients' place, we know how it would feel to lose someone, to lose their love, to be hurt, to be disapproved of, and the like.

People are mad, sad, and scared (Rako & Mazer, 1980). If we're talking about something else with a patient, we're usually just having a chat. Putting yourself in someone else's shoes is part of what I enjoy about the therapeutic process, because it helps me understand people. For me, understanding someone, and the growth of my understanding about them, is the part of this process that I enjoy the most.

Some people may be more naturally empathic than others. But I believe that one's empathic skills grow with experience, as well. The more people we sit with, I believe, the richer and more complex our capacity for empathy will be. The accumulation of our own life experiences can also contribute to our empathic skills.

Part of empathic work with people involves attempting to feel the pain that they're feeling, since one of our missions as therapists is to *understand pain in the service of relieving it.*

Using our *beginning* sessions with a patient, what does empathy tell us that they might be thinking and feeling initially? People think and feel a variety of things simultaneously. It would seem natural for them to be thinking about their symptoms and about the pain that has brought them to you. There's a hope that you'll be able to provide them with the relief they seek.

What else does empathy tell us about those beginning moments and beginning sessions? My sense is that, in a first session or sessions, the patient wonders about you as well as the treatment. He or she may also be uncomfortable verbalizing these concerns. *Is this therapist safe? Will I get the help I need? Will I be understood? Will I like this new therapist or not?* In first sessions, earlier experiences in treatment and beginning transference reactions are already causing people to be predisposed toward reactions to us in various ways. A patient in these opening moments might easily feel anxiety in discussing personal, sensitive, intimate details of his life with a stranger.

Analogously, what does our empathy toward a beginning therapist tell us about what she feels in opening sessions? A new therapist experiences a corresponding anxiety to that of the patient. *Who is this person I'm about to meet? Will I be able to help them? Will I like them? Will my "newness" be apparent?* Many of these questions will go unspoken as the door opens and the session begins.

It may be quite inappropriate for a therapist to share his or her anxiety with a patient. Why? Empathy tells us that such a disclosure might heighten the patient's anxiety. This point leads me to state another principle of conducting psychotherapy. It's an obvious one, but let's state it anyway. *Always do what's in the patient's best interest.* That should help keep you on the right track.

A new therapist's ability to help the patient "settle down" and feel calmer, listened to, and understood paves the way for the therapeutic plane to get off the ground.

Analytic listening

As we sit with patients, we're receptive and open to listening to anything. An attitude of interest in what's being said, felt, and communicated is a basic part of listening. Freud recommended an approach toward listening that he referred to as "evenly suspended attention" (Freud, 1912e). My understanding of this concept is a relaxed attunement towards the patient, without agenda, which allows the tool of analytic technique to be used. Fenichel wrote that this tool of analytic technique "is the unconscious of the analyst/therapist which intuitively comprehends the unconscious of the patient. Its aim is to lift this comprehension out of intuition into scientific clarity" (Fenichel, 1941, pp. 12–13, as cited in Jacobs, 1991, p. xiii).

In effect, I understand evenly suspended attention as listening in a relaxed way with no agenda so that anything the patient says can resonate with our own unconscious, thereby providing insight, connections, and understanding of the person with whom we're sitting.

All human beings have unconscious "radar" and, through it, can discern elements of the other. Part of the pleasure and creativity of our field is that we're not inspecting "the mind of the patient with remote detachment, like a scientist peering at the contents of a test tube" (Jacobs, 1991, p. xiii). We make use of the thoughts, feelings, and fantasies that occur within us as we listen.

Those thoughts, feelings, and fantasies are influenced by countless elements. Visual contact with a patient provides additional clues to the patient's unconscious. Facial expressions, body posture, and other non-verbal elements are particularly rich sources of information about the patient's unconscious. We do the work of listening with all of our senses. Our eyes and ears inform our unconscious radar as we attempt to think and feel what it's like to be the other we sit with. Learn to listen to your own thoughts, feelings, and fantasies, because your own associations further this process.

By monitoring ourselves, we also learn about the interaction between patient and therapist and about various aspects of ourselves. Awareness and attunement to these aspects of ourselves as part of a therapeutic dyad reveal much about what's going on within the patient, the therapist, and the complicated conscious and unconscious processes that take place between both. For example, I may find myself thinking of a dream my patient had years ago, something I saw in a movie, or a personal experience. Listening and attending to these thoughts and feelings helps us understand the person we're sitting with. This self-monitoring may involve feelings that you've become aware of, i.e., feeling angry, sexually excited, or bored. You can use these feelings to understand subtle dynamics between you and your patient and, ultimately, use this knowledge to elucidate the increasingly rich unconscious fabric of the person with whom you're working. In the process, you will also uncover material about yourself.

I have found my awareness of what I'm thinking, feeling, and fantasizing about to be a source of enormous insight into the patient, myself, and the unique interactional elements that occur between patient and therapist. This awareness is not a static phenomenon.

Those thoughts and feelings change, and I find my attunement to them invariably helpful to my understanding (Jacobs, 1991).

The awareness offered by analytic listening is one of the most creative and pleasurable aspects of our multidimensional work. As you uncover each layer, you can discern more and more about the patient, your unique interaction, and yourself.

Educating the patient

Let's return to our metaphor of the treatment as flying a plane. We have certain responsibilities as "flight instructors" in order to help the treatment take off. One of these responsibilities includes the therapist's role as educator. At the start of a treatment, the therapist may explain to the patient various aspects of the treatment, including why we're doing certain things and how a patient, as "co-pilot," actually has certain tasks that differ from their everyday modes of interacting.

Psychotherapy may feel to novice patients like a strange and different venture. One reason for this is that much of it varies from what takes place in normal interaction. It's helpful and important to educate the people with whom we're beginning to work on why we do some of the strange things we do. For example, why are therapists sometimes silent? Silence may be used at one point or another in a session, as we've discussed, to promote a helpful therapeutic regression. Patients new to psychotherapy may be perplexed as to why we're silent. Therefore, it may be sensible, and more empathic, to let a novice patient know that we're not silent in order to be mean but that, instead, it's actually for the benefit of the treatment—for their benefit.

To revisit our discussion regarding abstinence and anonymity, similarly, if we're not answering a patient's questions, we might explain that we're doing that for a specific purpose. A therapist might explain it this way: "Answering questions in certain instances can cut off thoughts, feelings, and fantasies that people have about me, but those things can actually be very useful to the treatment. Therefore, in order not to interfere with the treatment, I may not answer certain questions at times." This approach fosters and allows the regression to develop and continue. It allows anonymity, mystery, and ambiguity to begin in a reasonable and empathic manner.

Educating patients on their jobs

Early on in a treatment, I ask patients to say everything they're thinking and feeling while in the course of the therapy. I add that those things they find hard to say, we'll try to understand together. I share that I generally find those difficult thoughts quite important. After all, it's hard to say those things that are uncomfortable. What brings people to us is their pain. The urge to avoid pain is natural and inevitable. One of the most important tasks of a treatment, however, is to pursue pain (we'll be discussing this topic later on.) The thoughts, feelings, and fantasies a patient finds *uncomfortable* are the surface manifestation of pain and, thus, tend to be highly important.

There are all kinds of ways of avoiding pain. Silence on the part of a patient is one of them, and is a frequent phenomenon. But "the mind, like the heart, never stops" (Rako & Mazer, 1980, p. 71). I point this reality out to patients. I find silence to be an enactment of a defense against pain. Therefore, I try to help people understand what they're feeling during their periods of silence and then work with these moments to achieve new insights about what they may be avoiding.

***

Patients actually have two basic jobs. One job, which we've been describing, is to say everything that goes through their minds. The second job is more subtle and may initially be harder for them to understand. It's the task of listening to themselves. This listening, *the task of self-observation,* has various dimensions. It involves a cooperative venture with us in what we do as therapists. Self-observation involves patients in the process of hearing how they sound, making connections, and recognizing patterns in their thought processes. It is a sophisticated venture that helps them join us in the process of listening. Its encouragement by a therapist, and its pursuit, helps to solidify the therapeutic alliance, and it is interconnected with that aspect of the treatment. As patients listen to themselves and learn from it, they're able to say, "I'm doing it again," "I just stayed away from this," or, "I'm repeating this pattern." This task of self-observation can be encouraged by a therapist as he enlists his patient's help in the mutual task of listening. I believe it can grow as a treatment grows, but it can be fostered from the onset of a treatment.

A therapist may point out an infinite number of patterns, i.e., "I never hear you refer to your father," or, "Each time you mention Helen, I notice you seem more emotional." The patient may begin to notice these patterns and recognize them in themselves on their own. Enlisting the patient in the *self-listening task* asks the patient to join you in the analytic venture and to join in the process of listening. Through self-listening and self-observation, a patient's own ability to work in the treatment grows, and their insight grows, too.

I've used a metaphor to encourage patients and help them understand this process. I'll ask them to use their minds like a TV screen, and to say *everything* that comes up on the screen. This metaphor has a way of concretizing those tasks that can be hard to understand and follow. It helps people to say everything, as well as to watch themselves, as they say it.

Educating about cure: How treatment works

I also try to help patients understand how the process of psychotherapy works. People are frequently confused as to why "just talking" about something will produce a cure. I may, if I think it will be helpful to the cause, provide various explanations and well-known metaphors to explain.

When a new patient is confused by his or her symptoms, I've found it helpful to use the metaphor of their feeling like a boxer in a dark ring. They don't know who their opponent is, what they're up against, where to move, or how to counter. I'll explain that the job of therapy is to put the lights on to see what they're up against. I typically don't add (because it sounds too hokey), but have thought to myself, that a therapist will be with them in their corner, as well.

I'll also provide Freud's archeological metaphor with regard to symptoms. I'll explain that, during an archaeological dig, relics found underground can be preserved and remain relatively intact after many centuries. However, when exposed to light and air, those perfectly preserved relics begin to disintegrate. I'll go on to note Freud's original comment that symptomatic cure works in a similar way: once the history, roots, and unconscious meanings of a symptom are exposed through this process, they're also able to disintegrate. Both the archeological metaphor and the boxer metaphor use Freud's topographic theory of the mind: *Making the unconscious conscious.*

I've also found it useful to explain the notion of *cure* to those I'm working with, using Freud's later explanation of cure (through the structural hypothesis): namely, *"Where id was, ego shall be."*

I'll translate this into simple terms, for many reasons. One of these reasons is that I believe the unconscious talks in simple terms, i.e., hit, kill, grab, get, fuck. Sounds blunt, doesn't it? The unconscious *is* blunt. I also try to avoid making the treatment too intellectual. The people we work with need to understand what's happening on a gut level. We'll discuss this notion further in the next section, as well.

Regarding, "Where id was, ego shall be," I'll explain that the more insight people develop about the unconscious (the id, which I sometimes refer to as their "child side"), the stronger the ego, which I frequently call the "rational side," becomes.

On listening II: Learning to understand and cure

One of the most important tasks in the therapeutic process is something inherent in what we've been discussing. Your main job, as you listen, is to understand. Understanding grows as you sit with patients. The longer you sit with them trying to understand, the more understanding grows. The more you understand, the more you can help your patient to understand. That understanding should become mutual, and leads to an "aha!" That understanding produces symptom relief and character changes as both of you understand together. Relief of symptoms and character change generally lead to feeling better. If this improvement isn't taking place, you need, once again, to *understand* what's going on and what's going "wrong" to prevent understanding, growth, mastery, and symptom relief.

There is no substitute for simply sitting with patients over time. The more you do this, the more the process I've just described takes place. You grow, as well, since your understanding has increased, which helps you assist your patients even more in the future, in addition to assisting others like them.

Once again, we're all the same inside. People think and feel similar things. Our feelings and thoughts are never identical, but they can be pretty close. We make use of things we think and feel to understand the people we're working with. For this reason, empathy and the empathic process are integral to both listening and intervening. Our use of empathy allows us to understand what the other is thinking and feeling, which we can then put into words—ideally in a way that is sensitive, thoughtful, helpful, and *expansive of the other's awareness of himself.*

On resistance

One of the things we listen for from moment one is *resistance*. I think of resistance as anything that interferes with the progress and process of treatment. Resistance, as an expression of avoidance, is universal and ubiquitous, and needs to be listened for from the onset of treatment.

Conscious and unconscious resistances to working in a treatment exist throughout the treatment. However, people are different in their expression of resistance. Some patients cancel with the first flake of snow in the air, while others trudge to your office through two feet of snow. Some will cancel at the first hint of a scratchy sore throat, while others will arrive with a 102-degree fever.

When a patient first calls and asks, "Do you take U.S. Healthcare?" one thought I have is that they're already looking for the door. That's not to say that there aren't legitimate reasons for questions about the fee or insurance coverage on a person's mind, but I'm aware of the reverberation of resistance that's simultaneously present. Resistance is always there. It can take subtle forms, as with brief moments of silence when a patient holds back from saying what's on his or her mind. Alternatively, resistance can be enormous and dramatic, such as a sudden discontinuation of a treatment. It can take an infinite number of forms.

A therapist would be wise to attend to resistance and to engage it sensitively, respectfully, and appropriately as evidence of it becomes palpable. Helping your patient to observe and work through resistance is the next step.

Along those lines, I also keep my eyes and ears on distance and closeness with patients from the beginning. How close to me are they? Are they moving away? Do I feel them moving away from me? Distancing is a version of resistance that I always find myself monitoring throughout the course of a treatment.

Part of the therapeutic alliance involves mutual cooperation in seeing the task through, despite the inevitable internal and external resistances that arise. The therapeutic alliance can be particularly important during times of increased resistance and can help bridge times of increased resistance, including times when it feels like the bridge is about to be destroyed. Understanding resistance is, once again, central to engaging it and dealing with it.

Elements of conscious or unconscious resistance may be based on painful material, empathic failures on our part, a patient's own internal neurotic problems, or other complicated issues. The alliance, and the maintenance of the alliance, can prevent the treatment from being temporarily or permanently ended as both participants endeavor to understand, work with, and manage whatever resistance has surfaced at the time.

Following the affect

One of the most important things we're attending to, listening to, watching for, and trying to experience is the affect of the person we're sitting with. Affect is the expression of conscious or unconscious feeling. It is demonstrated in a multitude of ways. One of the reasons I find affect so important is that affects are close to the unconscious. I find affect to be the heart of a session and the heart of a person's life (Rako & Mazer, 1980). I notice a glint of a tear, a tremble in a cheek. I notice a grimace, an embarrassed smile, a sad smile, a momentary frown, surprise. As I notice it, I frequently explore it. In Malcolm Gladwell's (2005) book *Blink*, psychologists Paul Ekman and Wallace Friesen recognized 3,000 different measurable facial expressions! Become an expert at reading faces. Watch them. I find that sometimes a facial expression can tell me more than a thousand words. Notice the subtle changes, as well as the more obvious ones, to understand where your patient is at.

One of the advantages of psychotherapy (as opposed to analysis) is that the therapist has more contact with the patient's facial features and body posture than an analyst typically does in psychoanalysis, where a patient lies in a recumbent position. Patients' faces and bodies tell us a great deal about what they're feeling. Though facial expressions and body positions are closer to the unconscious than spoken words, words are, of course, also important in understanding affect. Subtle nuances of affect can be conveyed in the choice of different words. Tone of voice, as well, conveys what one is feeling.

Learn to follow affect, to track it. Sense what it is, when it changes, and how it changes. Is it particularly intense? Is it too intense? What do you notice about what they're feeling? Affect is something that should be tracked throughout the course of a treatment. Affect is an extremely important marker of what needs to be focused on, attended to, and sensitively mentioned to the person with whom you're sitting.

"Off-Key" notes

Another important marker for listening and intervening is what I call "off-key notes." What I mean by that confusing phrase is anything coming from a patient that sounds or feels *off-key*, i.e., odd, bizarre, strange, neurotic, out of sync, illogical, and the like. A particular affect might seem to be too intense or too understated for the situation. You might feel that something a patient decides to do seems strange or unusual. Pay close attention to these notes and, when in doubt, ask about and explore them. If something in their history seems unclear, sounds strange, or feels odd, don't be shy about asking. There are as many off-key notes as there are melodies, and they can manifest as peculiar responses, odd decisions, confusing behavior, paradoxical behavior or comments, or self-defeating actions. The list is endless.

A minor event or seemingly innocuous comment, inside or outside the treatment, may enrage your patient. Alternatively, a patient may exhibit little reaction to something major. At times, an off-key note may be as loud and obvious as an elephant sitting on a piano. At other times you may discern a note that is only slightly discordant with other things you know about the person with whom you're working. Frequently, these subtle discordant notes are signs of symptoms or conflicts that provide useful markers of issues and themes worth exploring.

Patterns

One easy way of intervening, especially early on in a treatment, is to identify themes and patterns. Patterns are important, and can be particularly useful in intervening. Let's say a patient you're starting to work with routinely begins to arrive five minutes late. Instead of remarking on it the first time, it is easier, more tactful, and more useful to wait until it happens more than once, then note that you've begun to notice a pattern of lateness to sessions and that you're curious about it. As you can see, these guideposts overlap—in this case, between patterns and how resistance might be handled.

Keeping self esteem in mind

One of the other principles to keep in mind is that, when you intervene, empathy demands that you be respectful of the self-esteem of the person with whom you are working. Using the previous example, if you're commenting on lateness, it needs to be done in such a way that your comment conveys curiosity about it or interest in learning about it, as opposed to being critical of the pattern—i.e., "You're late too often." Responding critically is also less neutral.

Typically, you want to avoid being critical, since a criticism can be experienced by a patient as judgmental and potentially hurtful. Being critical can interfere with the atmosphere of freedom we're trying to create with patients; therefore, it can interfere with a thorough and honest understanding of the issue or pattern at hand.

Going after pain

Patients come to us because they are in pain. They may not be conscious of it and it may be disguised in their symptoms, but pain is there nevertheless. One way of understanding what we're doing as therapists is that we're *going after pain*. We're attempting to understand the nature of the pain—its dimensions, its magnitude, and where it came from. We sit with people in order to help them bear pain, which is one of the comforts and gratifications that a treatment provides. Another perspective about treatment is that we help people in their pursuit of personal truth, which includes facing parts of themselves and their backgrounds that they find painful. This joint task is a difficult quest.

Painful thoughts and feelings tend to be more important than other thoughts and feelings, because the work that we're doing involves finding and exploring pain in order to relieve it. One surface manifestation of pain is discomfort. When a patient evidences discomfort, hesitance, or awkwardness—whether with a comment, a facial gesture, a tear, or perhaps a pause—it could seem to indicate that pain is close behind. Once it's picked up by our radar, the next task is attempting to understand that pain. We investigate it, helping our patients understand it and discover where it comes from, and in the end, hopefully, master it. We sit with patients until their pain goes away (Rako & Mazer, 1980).

Detective work

In reading Freud's cases as an early analytic candidate, I saw him at times as a detective investigating clues—clues found in his patients, in symptoms, in dreams, and in their histories.

I believe that we therapists do a kind of detective work; however, this work shouldn't involve interrogating the witness on the stand. Dragging a confession out of someone with relentless, clever, and cruel questions might result in police-like fact-gathering. In a therapy situation, however, that approach will fail. Interrogative detective work without the constant guidance of empathy will not produce a healthy, productive treatment; patients, especially masochistic ones, will "spill the beans" and "confess" when the confession may not even be accurate. Without the use of consistent empathy, used analytically over time, some kind of sado-masochistic version of treatment will form. For this reason, confrontation has its place in treatment, but it must be used cautiously and judiciously.

The three areas of mental content

Patients will talk about things in three different areas of mental life. They'll talk about 1) current outside reality, 2) the past, and 3) the treatment and transference. I separate transference and treatment, since many aspects of the treatment are not transference. Frequently, certain of these areas will tend to get left out, go untalked about, or be minimized.

It's generally easiest for patients to begin talking about current reality. That's a natural thing for people to do. Being a good therapist involves being a weaver, working back and forth between all three areas. Generally, those areas the patient doesn't talk about have something conflictual or defensive about them, bits of painful discomfort. In other words, if someone constantly talks about their current day boss or their spouse but rarely refers to their background and childhood, something defensive is operating about the past. A therapist, therefore, would be wise to listen for, attend to, and, at an appropriate point, intervene by noticing aloud that the patient avoids mentioning their background or certain elements of it. The same thing is true regarding a patient who rarely refers to the treatment. Certain thoughts, feelings, and fantasies about the treatment are similarly being avoided and, at some appropriate point, a therapist can point out this avoidance of the treatment to the patient.

Treatment as a listening focus

Another important focus in analytic listening is listening with an ear to references to the treatment and transference. It may be hardest for patients to talk directly about you and the treatment. But this needs to be—and should be—a focus for listening, particularly when it comes to unspoken negative thoughts or feelings about the therapist or therapy. For example, if a patient is talking about another doctor they dislike, or someone else they feel isn't helping very much, it may be easier for the therapist to collude with the patient by not addressing how this theme may indirectly refer to the patient's disgruntlement with the therapist or the therapy. A therapist would be wise to keep an ear tuned for disguised references to the treatment or transference that are only alluded to indirectly through these kinds of outside displacements. The issues which emerge in a patient about the treatment and transference have a unique place in treatment. They give an "in vivo," immediate, and direct understanding for the issues that brought a person to treatment as they unfold before your eyes. The way a patient distorts you as a result of transference can be uniquely helpful in making more evident to patients the source of difficulties they are having in relationships, as well as symptoms and character troubles they're experiencing outside the treatment.

Context and contiguity

Let's say my secretary (I don't actually have one) said to me, "Dr. Eichler, when are you going on vacation?" Without knowing the context within which this question has occurred, it's hard to know what my secretary is thinking. I'll go on to explain the context.

I've just said to her, "I need you to type 1,000 pages by the end of the day and to prepare several letters that I've already dictated. Oh, and I also need you to finish everything that I had given you yesterday as soon as possible."

At least one meaning of my secretary's question, "Dr. Eichler, when are you going on vacation?" becomes understandable when it's provided in a particular context. In the above case, of course, one meaning would be a weary secretary wishing for me to leave on vacation.

How about contiguity? Contiguity is the principle that things next to one another in thought are connected. Here's an example: An adolescent describes a conflictual wish. He's struggling with his parents' request that he drive their car only when they are present, since he has only a learner's permit that requires his parents' presence while driving. However, he wants to do it on his own anyway, and his friends are encouraging him to drive the car on a weekend when his parents are away. He decides to do it. He talks about feeling guilty because he disobeyed his parents. Right after taking the car, unaccompanied by his parents, a minor car accident ensues. The episode is described in that sequence by this adolescent patient. One might speculate that there would be a connection between the patient's guilt associated with taking the car and the accident that followed, especially if the two are described contiguously.

The lecture and the lab

Psychotherapy involves a continuous process of learning about oneself over time. Patients and therapists talk, and mutually try to understand, together. But there are times during the course of a treatment when talking must be translated into action in order for actual behavioral change to take place.

One of my patients, Mr. E., whom I will discuss later in the book, had symptoms of what he and I together labeled "Stu and Alan syndrome." This funny way of describing symptoms came from a history that E. had of never saying "no" to a plan or a person. Stu and Alan were two of his friends in early high school. Come Saturday night, Stu and E. would discuss going to a movie. E. would say to Stu, "I'll go to that movie with you." Later on, however, when E. learned of Alan's plans to accompany some girls to an amusement park, he'd tell Alan he'd go with him. In effect, Mr. E. presented a pattern of promising a commitment to two people, and at the last minute saying "no" to one and choosing the more appealing option. E. did the same thing with plans, friends, girlfriends, and, ultimately, his wife. His presenting symptom involved a history of womanizing and affairs during his marriage, which broke up because of it. He had been "a two-woman man" for most of his life, but this behavior also took the form of committing to conflicting plans or visions in multiple areas of his life.

Interestingly, when Mr. E. began treatment with me, he was simultaneously in another treatment that he found too supportive and directive. He told me he'd be ending it with his other therapist, but even though he talked about ending the other treatment with "Judy," he continued seeing her for a while during his treatment with me.

"Stu and Alan syndrome" involved multiple problems that Mr. E. and I began to work on. One problem was that Mr. E. wanted to have it all. He sought to avoid sustaining any loss by, in effect, not making a definitive decision. Of course, Mr. E.'s syndrome also involved a problem with honesty, as well as grandiosity—he believed that he could "get away with it."

The metaphor of "the lecture and the lab" means that treatment can't just be approached as a lecture, an interesting intellectual exercise devoid of any outside work. Indeed, new understanding and change need to be worked on in the "lab" of the outside world. The insights derived from a treatment must be put into action outside the treatment, as well.

E. knew that his "Stu and Alan syndrome" was wrecking his life. It had ruined his marriage and was ruining other parts of his life, including friendships and work relationships. Others would, of course, ultimately recognize his duplicity and then see E. as a dishonest scoundrel, someone who made promises and didn't deliver on them.

Mr. E. talked about the lab work in which he engaged after his marriage broke up, in which he did not promise exclusivity to a girlfriend if he wasn't being exclusive. I explained to him that one of the advantages of doing this kind of lab work was that through his avoidance of old patterns—by refusing to engage in his previous pattern of duplicitous actions—we would gain further access to thoughts, feelings, and fantasies that were getting lost because of his repetitive, self-destructive enactments.

As we worked on these patterns in the treatment, he began to do the lab work of actually giving up his "Stu and Alan" behaviors outside the treatment. He stopped the duplicitous dating of two "exclusive girlfriends" at a time. Through his lab work of stopping this behavior, he began to become aware of other elements of the "Stu and Alan syndrome" of which he had been unconscious. He felt vulnerable and uncomfortable about having "all his eggs in one basket," for example. However, through the work in both the lecture (the treatment) and the lab (his outside efforts at changing), this old symptomatic pattern gradually improved.

Mr. E. also finally gave up "Judy," the other therapist, and allowed his eggs to be gathered in one treatment basket. Without doing work in both areas, inside and outside the treatment, in both the lecture and the lab, I believe this man's symptoms would have continued to wreak havoc on his life. As he enjoyed the feeling of being a more upstanding man, he felt better, became more assertive, and gave up self-punitive behaviors that had arisen from guilty feelings.

Intervening

The process of listening and understanding is a natural part of the process that leads to intervention. As a result, it is somewhat artificial to separate these therapeutic functions, because they are interwoven with each other.

As you listen to and understand a patient, new awarenesses form in your mind about the person that you're sitting with. We try to take these awarenesses or insights and put them into words. Of course we're making use of empathy—including our concern for dosage, tact, and timing—to guide us. Certain things that may occur to us about someone may be correct, but timing might dictate that your patient is not ready to hear them. Alternatively, certain thoughts might be idiosyncratic, or too revealing about you, to make use of for the purposes of an intervention.

As therapists, we're trying to expand the insight and understanding of the person with whom we're working. Listening and intervening are intertwined with one another. Indeed, as a therapist listens, and as thoughts, fantasies, and impulses come to his or her mind, the therapist may begin to shape an insight that can be offered to a patient. Not infrequently, it's easier for a beginning therapist to offer a tentative question, but with more experience and understanding, more declarative comments can be made that enlarge and enrich the understanding of the person with whom you're working.

Everything that we've been discussing thus far—as well as everything that we have yet to discuss—informs your ability as a therapist to understand your patient and, ultimately, to put that understanding into words. All of the guideposts discussed in this text naturally lead to further understanding of what is taking place in your patient's psyche. As a result, they become guideposts for intervening as well as for listening.

As I mentioned before, Fenichel said that the most important tool the analyst has is his own unconscious (Fenichel, 1941, as cited in Jacobs, 1991, p. xiii). All human beings have a kind of unconscious radar. We can pick up, discern, and understand things about people we're with by using a host of different cues. We do our work with ears and eyes, allowing thoughts and feelings to come to our minds. These cues give us a virtually infinite amount of information about our patients. A central part of our work is to put these thoughts into words, which produce *interpretations*. Our understanding grows in dimension and depth the longer we sit with our patients. The interpretations we provide further the process of regression and lead to new associations.

> "Interpretation is the central activity of the analyst during treatment—a process whereby the analyst expresses in words what he or she comes to understand about the patient's mental life. This understanding includes aspects of psychic life that were formerly unconscious or known to the patient only in an incomplete, inaccurate, or otherwise distorted form. Interpretation is also based upon observation of the way the patient distorts the relationship with the analyst to meet unconscious needs and to relive old experiences.
>
> An interpretation is the statement of new knowledge about the patient. Both patient and analyst may contribute to it, although it is usually initiated by the analyst.
>
> The process of interpretation usually involves additions and modifications by both analyst and patient as new material

emerges. That process allows the patient to understand his or her past and present inner life in a new, less distorted, more complete way, leading to the possibility of changes in feeling, attitude, and behavior." (Moore & Fine, 1990, pp. 103–104).

The process of interpretation is a central technique that the therapist uses to deepen a treatment and further the regression.

Therapists use other, more supportive interventions including advice, suggestion, and direction. It is possible that a psychotic, or very low-functioning, person may need more direct guidance and advice. A therapist in those circumstances is, in effect, functioning as an auxiliary ego. The techniques we discussed in allowing a regression to take place need to be limited or used judiciously with more severely ill people who may have trouble with regression and can be too regressed already in their functioning.

Such a caveat does not hold true with healthier, higher-functioning people. Let's return to an example from earlier in the text—namely, the woman who was having trouble asserting herself with her boss. One type of intervention would be telling her what to do and say, advising her on the words to use in her interaction, and the like. As we discussed, one of the problems with this kind of "supportive" approach—i.e., being told what to say—is that patients may lose the opportunity to learn more about themselves and deepen the treatment. Other problems also arise with this kind of "supportive" advice-giving. In addition to fostering dependence, therapists who use this approach set themselves up as a kind of seer, a sort of Delphic oracle, whose advice-giving guidance is needed for the patient to function. Such a pivotal position may gratify a therapist's narcissistic needs, as well as a patient's conscious or unconscious need for dependence and even masochistic control.

Our examination of these issues highlights some of the differences between an "insight-oriented" versus "supportive" psychotherapy approach. Yet there is frequently an overlap between the two: I've found that many times *the best way of being supportive is to offer a good interpretation.*

SECTION IV

"OUR PATIENTS ARE OUR TEXTBOOKS": LESSONS FROM CLINICAL CASES (RAKO & MAZER, 1980)

CHAPTER NINE

Patient A.: Educating about cure

"A." was a 25-year-old architect who presented after his first marriage broke up. He was devastated by the divorce, but the couple had known that A. had a "problem." They rarely had sex, and A. intimated to his wife that he was interested in other men. His wife "suddenly" left after a four-year marriage.

A. was traumatized. He thought he loved her, but knew he was not very interested in her sexually, despite her attractiveness. A. had been aware of his attraction to other men since junior high school; however, he said that he had a heterosexual identity and felt "like a man." His own sense of masculine identity was very different from other gay men I've treated over the years.

He very much wanted to be married, wished to have children, and was, in fact, desperate to attain these goals in reality. The breakup of his marriage was a terrible blow that left him reeling and questioning whether he could ever succeed in obtaining his wish.

A.'s mother died of cancer when he began middle school. He remembered a sense of numbness around the time of her death. He recalled the traumatic day when it became clear that she was about to die. He needed to be prodded by his father to "tell her you love her." He did so, dutifully.

A. was an altar boy, literally and figuratively. Both of his parents were very religious, but he recalls feeling like an automaton, engaging in religious and academic rituals at parochial school dutifully and numbly. He recalled never having a mind of his own, never disagreeing, never having opinions, and still felt this way into his adulthood.

His father was a gruff, self-involved transit police officer who coached many sports but never coached his own son in any sport. At family gatherings, A. felt more comfortable "hanging out with the girls." He was an awkward athlete and never recalled being helped or encouraged to improve by his father, who told him he should be a priest. Rare heterosexual forays in early adolescence, like putting his hand on Mary Caraca's thigh in a dress shop basement, were discovered and actually broken up by his "detective" father who "caught them" when they were together. His father told him, "Get out of there and get home."

In addition to being an altar boy, A. played in the parochial school band. The worst part of this was "band camp." He described this summer program for kids in the band as "an Auschwitz" of playing endless, monotonous songs in ninety-degree heat.

A.'s father would lead the family regularly in praying the rosary at home. When A.'s older brother Anthony rebelliously objected and left to go upstairs, their father pursued him, quickly and viciously banging his head against the wall, telling him, "Get back and pray with everyone else."

His mother's death when A. was fourteen followed her diagnosis of cancer by about a year. His father's quick involvement with a new woman and rapid remarriage deepened the sense of disconnection from his father. The father himself had serious problems with relatedness prior to the illness and loss of his wife.

A. recalled through childhood and adolescence a chronic sense of being "almost invisible" when it came to his father. He recalled his father's attitude toward him as indifferent, bored, and distant; his father flipped channels on TV without any discussion between them when they were in the same room. Occasionally, A.'s father asked him to accompany him for a ride to get cigarettes. These were empty, wordless rides, with A. feeling like a prop to keep his father company.

A.'s mother, a quiet librarian, was a warmer figure who seemed overwhelmed by her life. Five children and a bullying, narcissistic husband left her depressed. A. recalled being in church with his mother, who lingered after the service, her hands over tear-filled eyes.

One way A. received attention was through his academic performance: his mother praised him for being an excellent student. However, when A. told his father he wanted to go to graduate school in architecture and asked his father for financial assistance to help him afford graduate school, his father replied, "Well, I guess you won't be an architect."

The primary contact between father and son took a very particular and meaningful form. On many nights after dinner, his father asked A. and his older brother Anthony to help bathe him in his bathroom. The baths had a ritualistic quality to them; A. recalled more detail as the treatment proceeded. The father was naked in the tub as his sons scrubbed his feet, legs, and back. A. recalled a washcloth "floating over his genitals."

The father asked his sons to clip his toenails and blow his hair dry. He complimented them on their service, one of the few compliments A. seemed to receive. Although A. didn't recall exactly when these baths began, he speculated that he was around seven or eight, and recalled that they went on intermittently for years.

A. experienced much stimulation (at the time unconscious) during these bath scenes, and certain aspects of the bathing ritual were repeated and re-enacted in later life. One precipitant to the break-up of A.'s first marriage involved his awareness of sexual stimulation while in public bathrooms upon glimpsing other penises and having his own penis looked at. One homosexual enactment that had taken place prior to his marriage was an encounter in an architectural school bathroom (the bathroom, looking, and touching being an obvious and significant part of the repetition). A. also experienced brief and infrequent homosexual contact with a neighbor during early high school.

"Penis hunting," as he called it, became a frequent and conflictual activity following the break-up of his first marriage. This activity consisted of going to public bathrooms in search of a glimpse of a penis or an encounter, typically consisting of mutual felatio. This activity lasted quite some time. All the while A. felt conflicted, ashamed, and guilt-ridden about this, yet he remained positive he wanted to meet, marry, and have children with a woman he loved.

Ultimately, he met a woman whom he felt he genuinely cared about, but he was still troubled by new symptoms, which involved meeting young men on the internet and having sexual encounters with them. He struggled with the question, "Will I ever really be done with these feelings?" He wondered whether he was really gay and just fooling himself.

I didn't have the answers to those questions, but the symptoms and symptomatic enactments began slowly to resolve over time. Getting back to "Where id was, ego shall be," one of A.'s first changes was putting an end to the penis hunting. His frustration-tolerance and impulse-control matured. Bathroom encounters and returns to the "scene of the crime" stopped altogether. These changes occurred after several years of our attempting to understand all of what he had talked about in his past, his current reality, and their dimensions and links to his feelings about the treatment and transference.

However, one of the easiest ways for A. to meet men, as mentioned, became the internet. A. called talking to them "chatting," and the encounters he called "cheating." Though at this point much older, he claimed to be more than a decade younger than he actually was. This symptom revealed that A. felt robbed of his youth and wanted to stay young forever. (His screen name implicitly indicated a younger man's name and age which, importantly, never changed despite the passage of years). A. felt that he had been robbed of his youth by having to grow up too quickly. After his mother's death, he had to take over household chores, many of which had been done by his mother and were stereotypically feminine, such as cooking and cleaning. This altar boy automaton felt dead; like his dead mother, he felt that he had never been allowed to "live," instead following rote, strict religious, academic, and social rules. His bad-boy encounters and enactments made him feel free, rebellious, alive, and young.

A.'s deepening understanding of all of these dynamics increased his rational side's capacity for impulse control. Highly dangerous and potentially self-destructive encounters ended. Some of these could have ended with an early death, like his mother—a similarity and repetition he began to understand.

A. decided to get engaged to his girlfriend, whom he loved, while he continued work on his sexual situation. The encounters briefly increased as a response to his child side unconscious, which seemed to say, "You may get engaged, but you'll never get me to be the perfect altar boy ever again."

All of these themes came further into A.'s consciousness, and we worked with them inside and outside the transference as genuine changes in his behavior and understanding seemed to take place. The encounters stopped. Remarkably, A. also stopped the "chatting and cheating," in which he had engaged for years on the computer.

A. got married. Importantly, the birth of his first child seemed to be another factor in his change. He was determined to be the antithesis of his own father. Indeed, he was quite involved in her care, feeding, diapering, and so on, despite the demands of his professional practice. The sublimation of becoming a father himself became an important "phallic achievement" for him and helped to solidify his masculine identification.

Interestingly, his actual awareness of homosexual excitement, in and of itself, began to diminish. I've worked with other people whose analogous sexual feelings didn't change, despite other changes made. He experienced a marked improvement in the sexual relationship with his new wife. This improvement seemed genuine and increasingly integrated within him. A. felt, as time went on, that he had changed as a result of the insights accumulated over a lengthy treatment that progressed over many years. I believe A.'s rational side became stronger and less impulsive, and that his masculine identification became far more solidified as a result of his lengthy analytic work.

Other interesting and important changes took place in A.'s rational side. A. had been invested in remaining a child—a result of his feeling that he had been robbed of the fun and excitement of childhood and adolescence. Initially, he had been invested in remaining childlike even to his own professional and personal detriment. On his way to my office, he'd see cars with high school boys in them, hats askew, laughing and enjoying themselves. He looked longingly at them, wishing to be one of them. Indeed, in certain ways he acted like them. He described one incident at work. There were bowls of licorice and candies at the front desk, which he'd "scamper over to." He recalls a secretary saying to him, "Looking for candy, little boy?" He would look for the various types of candy he had missed out on as a child. He also appeared to look like a younger boy early on in therapy; he spiked his hair, talked, dressed, and behaved in a manner befitting a teenager or young adult, though he was much older.

All of these tendencies changed gradually through the treatment. His rational side no longer wanted to be perceived as a kid, and he became uncomfortable with, and resentful of, comments such as, "Looking for candy, little boy?" in both professional and personal settings.

A. became more assertive. He understood that much of what had gone into being his father's "homosexual valet" was his only way of getting "good stuff" from his father. He wanted no part of that with current father figures. His anger, resentment, and rebelliousness toward his father early on played out transferentially toward me by withholding discussion of secret encounters—a phenomenon that we ultimately talked about and understood together. The transference rebelliousness of not telling me about these encounters ended as he realized what he was enacting, and that his behaviors were turning the treatment into a sham. He no longer allowed clients to keep him helplessly on the phone for hours, giving up the role of an altar boy who was there only to serve others.

The strands of the rope

In treatment, I make use of another of Freud's helpful metaphors in explaining how symptoms and insight work. Freud spoke of symptoms and cure using the metaphor of a boat tied to a dock with a rope. He explained that the rope is composed of a number of strands. Only when all of these strands are cut can the boat be freed to set sail.

The strands of the rope are the multiple factors (the principle of multiple determination) contributing to the production of symptoms. In order for A. to improve, he needed to understand the multiple issues that determined his sexual situation and other symptoms in order to cut the strands. A.'s sexual situation and other symptoms were composed of multiple strands, many of which were woven together. One of the strands of the rope that comprised A.'s strong feminine wishes was his overstimulation by his father's baths. The baths were a kind of sexual abuse, involving direct physically and visually stimulating contact with a man with whom A. deeply desired contact. They aroused curiosity and interest in "what was under the washcloth." These baths were one of the obvious historical antecedents of looking for penises in bathrooms. At times, A. and his brother also shared a bed and cuddled, provoking further homosexual stimulation for this affection-starved child. Both parents' relative paucity of emotional availability also led to this cuddling—another strand in the rope.

One of the important paths towards identification is loss, as Freud describes in *Mourning and Melancholia* (1916–1917g). A.'s feminine identification increased with the loss of his mother in early adolescence. His incorporation of her allowed her to stay within him as a part of him: he could cook like her or clean like her.

An early symptom he spoke of with me was a feeling of "deadness." This included a feeling that his "penis was dead" during sexual contact with his first wife. These symptoms also came to be understood, in part, as an identification with his dead mother.

His problem in identifying with his father was a particularly complicated part of his history. On the one hand, he yearned for his father's acceptance and closeness. On the other hand, the last kind of man he wanted to be like was his father—selfish, gruff, disconnected, abusive, someone who had bashed his son's head against the wall when he objected to prayer. Very importantly, the lack of interest his father showed him throughout his life—exemplified in his father's statement, "I guess you won't be an architect" and his lack of involvement with A.'s athletic development, together with other neglectful and poor treatment—contributed to A.'s disidentifying with the original man. *All of these factors, as well as others, were the multiple strands of the rope that contributed to A.'s sexual situation.* As his understanding of these strands grew, he grew and matured as a man. This increased understanding led to marked symptom relief, as well as significant character changes.

CHAPTER TEN

Patient B.: Encouraging self-observation

One of the most valuable and therapeutic tools used in treatment is *self-observation*. Self-observation involves encouraging the people we're working with to be co-investigators of themselves. In order for that to happen, in addition to the job of saying everything that comes to mind, I ask patients to *listen to themselves*. Intermittently, I might ask, "How does that sound?"

To further the task of self-observation, I'll refer to the ego as "your rational side," and I'll use certain metaphors in helping patients to self-observe their unconscious (their id). I'll provide another clinical example to illustrate this.

B., a 35-year-old banker, presented to treatment with certain painful symptoms. He was a respected, successful investment banker at a major firm. B. was wealthy, married, had two healthy, successful children, and, by most standards, had a good life. However, he was an extremely unhappy, embittered man. He suffered from much self-doubt about the quality of his work, and felt unrecognized.

He developed certain symptoms in adult life with which he struggled, and which ultimately brought him to treatment. The main symptoms were intrusive thoughts involving violence towards his wife, whom he consciously loved very much and to whom he was deeply devoted. His wife had a medical illness, which began to cause serious symptoms requiring many surgical procedures. She experienced frequent pain and multiple complaints for which the patient felt responsible for attending to and even curing.

B. began to develop symptoms consisting of "intrusive thoughts" of stabbing her with a knife, pushing her down a flight of stairs, and hitting her in the head with a phone. He felt enormously guilty and panicked over these thoughts, which he experienced as totally foreign, disgusting, horrifying, and from another world. In effect, they *were* emanating from another world—the world of his unconscious.

He had previously developed other symptoms, which had begun earlier in adult life. He was afraid of traveling, especially far away. He felt anxious about going on vacations. If he chose a vacation spot and the elements of the trip weren't perfect, he became very self-critical. If something as minor as a stain on the hotel room rug intruded, he grew morose, depressed, embittered, and enraged. Not seeing all the sights, or even not choosing the "right" place for breakfast, evoked massive self-criticism and rage.

Another set of symptoms was triggered by a physical symptom of his own. Once, while on a camping vacation and hiking on a trail, B. fainted, or possibly had a seizure. He had a medical work-up, but no medical cause for the episode was ever found. It never recurred, and neither the nature of the event nor the correct diagnosis was ever discovered.

This experience on the hike triggered tremendous anxiety in B. His anxiety on vacations increased, and new symptoms developed, as well. He became terrified of seizures and fainting, and suffered "brown-outs"—he'd "sense" some kind of dizziness or loss of consciousness and became terrified of fainting in public. No other fainting spell or seizure ever took place again, but the fear of it lasted for many years, extending into the treatment.

B. attempted to gain control over his fear through a self-made rule: "If I can still read something, I'm okay." This rule led to hurried attempts at reading something to reassure himself that he was not going to faint, or have a seizure, if he sensed a brown-out.

B. had been a serious child. His childhood seemed to have been dominated by reprimands and endless, repetitive, frequent fights with his bossy, serious, and critical father, a school principal. B. recalls his father saying absurdly critical things. For example, in response to his receiving a 98 on an exam, his father asked, "What happened to the other two points?" Childhood felt like an unending series of scenes in which he was told he was "wrong" by his father. He described his mother as a wimp who let this go on, a largely absent figure. He felt unprotected and badly let down by her.

B.'s childhood had a lonely, isolated quality to it. The oldest of three boys, he felt severely unrecognized, unrewarded, and diminished by that loneliness. He felt separate from his two younger brothers who shared a room. Serious, bookish, and very involved with rules, he recalled feeling enraged when his meticulously ordered Monopoly® cards were put out of place or his brothers changed the order of his comic books. He had trouble making friends, and was criticized by classmates when he reprimanded them for doing things "against the rules." Although an excellent student, he was accepted by a college that he deemed below his standards, and felt he deserved better.

One of B.'s first symptomatic "attacks" occurred on a trip to Europe in graduate school with two friends. He was lured into a game of three-card monty on a train and lost. He felt so humiliated and enraged by this that he began to think about suicide to the point that he briefly played with razor blades. The intensity of his child side's demand to be "right" and to win was assaulted and defeated, leading to a symptomatic regression.

This episode, along with other outbreaks of symptoms he experienced as an adult, I see as an example of what Freud termed "the return of the repressed." In effect, certain symptomatic, uncontrollable, repetitive thoughts and feelings became conscious as B. found himself in certain situations that activated memories of his troubled childhood, especially situations where he felt "wrong." B. had been locked in a fight to the finish with his father around "who was right and who was wrong," causing endless arguments and interpersonal war. More technically, experiences in adulthood re-evoked feelings from the original conflict, and the defenses against his aggression became overwhelmed, producing a symptomatic return of the repressed. Wishes to kill as well as the need for punishment and retaliation in kind for these urges emerged, producing intense anxiety. His vulnerable self-esteem was under constant attack by new reality, including a critical new boss who rarely provided "enough" recognition. B.'s unconscious (his child side) demanded perfect order, control, and realization of what he felt he deserved. Reality, it seemed, was not complying with this demand.

B.'s vulnerable self-esteem system produced a need for perfect rightness and control. His conscious understanding of this need was to protect himself from his father's relentless, critical attacks, which he internalized and directed at himself as well. When he fainted or had the seizure on the hike, he found he was not even in control of his own body. His wife's persistent medical symptoms were like a slap in the face in light of his wish for perfect control. Despite his love for her and devotion to her (indeed, his care and carefulness were far beyond normal standards), a part of him hated her and wanted her hurt and dead for her flaws—and thus his flaws, as well.

This enraged part of him was his unconscious, his child side. The child *demanded* perfect control, perfect order, and perfect results for all the effort he put in—this was the same child side that wanted his Monopoly® cards to be in order and his comic books perfectly lined up. At times when I spoke with B., I referred to his child side as "the kid."

I use the term *the kid* with B. and with other patients for several reasons. The unconscious, though hard to sum up with one metaphor, does display prominent aspects of childhood. These childhood residues result in symptoms and character traits with childhood elements—for example, what I've been describing in B.

As an actual "kid" in childhood, he was demanding, argumentative, and wanted his own way. The oldest of three brothers, he greatly identified with his kingly father, whom he referred to as "often wrong, but never in doubt." In the treatment and transference, his child side showed itself early on in endless arguments with me.

A bright child, B. liked to play games. He was a very good game player and valued his excellent mind. He referred to the treatment as a game—in particular, a chess match. The treatment became, for him, a battle of wits in which, at times, learning about himself (including self-observation) became secondary to winning some kind of argument, frequently one about a relatively trivial point. He referred to the treatment as "just a battle of competing ideas."

My own self-observations were very helpful in working with B. As he played out his "chess match" with me, I could sometimes feel myself entering into it with him. *My own self-observation of the tug-of-war within me to enter this chess match assisted* me in understanding what was taking place in certain sessions. My awareness of it helped me to interpret to him what he was doing, and added to my insight about him. B. had been a lonely boy with few playmates, and I realized that part of him wanted to engage me in "playing forever," finding a playmate in me to battle, play with, and defeat endlessly. As I interpreted it to him, he wanted to set things up so that he could endlessly win and avoid aloneness with his therapist—his new father, foe, and playmate.

We learned that, as a child, he had felt secretly angry and misunderstood. He felt hurt by, and angry at, his kingly, critical father with whom he incessantly argued. Additionally, he felt enraged at his mother for not protecting and siding with him: "A lion should protect her cubs," and she had not. He also felt angry at his brothers for excluding him, and his peers for not obeying or following his rules, and for, in fact, mocking him for his obsession with rules.

His angry kid side produced additional symptoms and symptomatic behaviors. He'd play variations on "chicken" with cars on the road. If cut off, he'd then cut them off or honk at people for not following traffic rules—a dangerous enactment of his war games and secret murderousness.

His kid side's sadism and murderousness became most evident to him in his intrusive thoughts. His rational side loved his wife and was extremely loyal and devoted to her. His intrusive thoughts of stabbing her with a knife seemed foreign, horrible, and otherworldly.

The process of helping him involved helping him to *self-observe* that this other world was part of his own inner world. Referring to his unconscious as "the kid" helped him to work with the world of his unconscious. It helped him observe it, study it, and, even though he had always known it came from him, begin to *accept* it as part of himself.

One of the insights that helped B. understand his child side came from a set of thoughts he had early on in treatment. He mentioned that he had had an interesting thought when thinking about intrusive thoughts of all kinds. He said he had had a "visual image of a kid in a sandbox suddenly, impulsively pushing another kid." This important image helped him to understand that an important context for these intrusive thoughts was childhood. As he thought about it, the intrusive thoughts felt like "a kid having a tantrum, doing something impulsively."

Working with his "kid" helped the intrusive thought symptoms to disintegrate and come under far better conscious control. As he learned about his kid side, he became less afraid of it and more in control of it. Other intrusive thoughts, like vaulting over a balcony at the Hyatt hotel, began to be understood as a "tantrum" expressed by his kid side when something at a hotel (too small a room, or a stained carpet) displeased him, as inevitably his perfectionistic and kingly kid side would be displeased—*l'enfant terrible*. The intrusive thought symptoms became understandable and far less frightening for him.

Interestingly, this metaphor of "the kid" separates out the unconscious into a discrete, observable phenomenon. Patients are able to look at it and "self-observe" it, and of course can still recognize that it's a part of themselves. Thus, I've found that the use of "the kid" as a metaphor helps patients to understand, and integrate their understanding of, the unconscious. It helps patients become more active self observers and furthers analytic therapeutic work. Indeed, Mr. B. became far less frightened of his unconscious. Ultimately, his understanding and new insights also helped the intrusive thoughts to disintegrate. When they occasionally appeared later on, he could comfortably recognize what produced them and recognize that it was just his "kid side" having a tantrum.

CHAPTER ELEVEN

Patient C.: Identifying themes and furthering understanding of how symptoms develop

At this point, I'll further develop my illustration of symptoms and their formation with another clinical example. I'll also explain how I make use of other metaphors in helping patients understand what's troubling them.

Mrs. C. was a 37-year-old hospital healthcare worker who presented to treatment after a lengthy previous treatment that she found unsuccessful. Mrs. C. had been extremely anxious for as long as she could remember. She felt uncomfortable with many aspects of her life. In addition to experiencing tension that seemed unbearable, she often felt depressed. At the outset of treatment, she told me that she felt she couldn't cope with her life and often wished she were dead.

She had multiple GI symptoms (diarrhea and constipation), she couldn't relax during sex with her husband or experience orgasm. Life frequently felt awful. She had few friends, difficulty making friends, frequent headaches, and a host of other complaints. Sleep was a problem. She felt discouraged by the lack of success of her previous treatment, but, to her credit, didn't want to give up.

Mrs. C. was the oldest of five children. She was her father's favorite, but she experienced her childhood as having had an animalistic quality to it. Her mother, overwhelmed by the number of children she had, had a limited capacity for empathy and was prone to violent episodes. The patient recalled her mother taking a nap in a summer cottage and telling the patient not to wake her. When C. quietly tiptoed into the bungalow with her older cousin, her mother awoke, enraged at being roused, and pushed the patient against the stair rail, causing a gash in C.'s leg. She also hit C. with wet towels when upset or sent C. off to her grandmother—a "punishment" at times experienced as a welcome respite from the chaos.

Her father's temper was legendary. He was always screaming at someone. The siblings also constantly fought, with too little "good stuff" (love and empathy) to go around. C. found her siblings intrusive and provocative. For example, her younger brother frequently touched her, tried to kiss her, and would unexpectedly burst into her room as she dressed or undressed. When C. complained about his behavior, her mother dismissed it, saying, "He just loves you," or, "Don't worry about it." Her younger sister took her clothing and medicine, and, even in adult life, kissed her on the lips to express "affection." This behavior was regularly dismissed by her mother, as well.

Her father seemed to favor her which took the form of flirtatious and teasing comments. He found her cute, and C. got a lot of attention from boys in general; however, if her father saw her playing tag too energetically with boys in the neighborhood, he accused her of being a "slut." On the other hand, the patient found her father taking naps in her bed intermittently. When C. was an adult, after her mother died, he would comment, "I wish I had a woman like you."

Once, while on a cross country trip, she and her sister, who were both in their late teens, were invited to a dance held by staffers at a national park. She recalls doing nothing sexual, but also recalls that on their return they were accused by their father of being sluts.

As an attractive young woman, she recalled receiving a great deal of pleasure and attention from boyfriends. She had many boyfriends early on, and married an appropriate boyfriend at a young age.

Her many anxiety symptoms, in all of their manifestations, had multiple causes. Mrs. C. was overstimulated aggressively and sexually. She experienced her childhood as a series of unending aggressive and sexual assaults. Someone—a parent or sibling—was always about to hit her, touch her, steal from her, or the like. Her mother might slap her with a towel. Her father might yell. Her sibling might burst into her room unexpectedly. Her sister would steal from her and hurt her. Even at current-day family gatherings, her sister still said provocative and unnerving things. For example, after the patient's husband had back surgery, her sister said, "My friend's husband had the same surgery; things have never been the same for them. It's horrible." On hearing this comment, Mrs. C. wondered, "This is supposed to make me feel better?"

One of the basic principles of psychological development, as well as symptom formation, is that the past determines the future. Since parents and siblings serve as the prototypes for future relationships, one of Mrs. C.'s neurotic compromises has been to avoid closeness. She is a bright, friendly woman who chats on store or movie lines with strangers, but has few friends. She has a handful of friends in other parts of the country. I've remarked to the patient in the treatment that it seems the only friends she has are people who live in different states. She laughed and agreed. Her need for geographic distance reflects an important underlying distrust and tension with everyone.

In the small house in which she grew up, sharing a room with her sister, C. had the sense that, "everyone was on top of everyone." Her siblings touched her, hit her, kissed her unexpectedly, and stole from her. Today, friends and family—indeed, people, in general—are not to be trusted. C. has worked with this issue inside and outside of the treatment. Her father's business dealings, even in adulthood, confirmed for her the validity of her feelings: he was in business with relatives who steal from each other and from the government. His boasts about "screwing" family members horrified and appalled her. When she helped out in the business, she felt sullied by it. A basic symptomatic attitude resulting from C.'s childhood was that the world is full of selfish, intrusive users. This mistrust of people was further confirmed when she became aware of her father's "sleazy" business dealings.

Sadly, some of the traumas of her childhood were compounded by, and repeated in, her earlier treatment. Her former psychotherapist seduced her, calling her his "girl" and, at some points, hugging her. It appeared, as we talked about it, that he used her for his own needs. Part of our work has included helping her understand her own gratifications of this "special treatment," which she was reluctant to leave. Nevertheless, she ended up feeling used by him, and sensed that she had been kept far too long in treatment, more for his benefit than for hers.

An important part of C.'s treatment with me has been identifying the strands of the tension rope and her own need to reproduce anxiety. This aspect of treatment involved her gaining a deep and full understanding of these past events and understanding their connection to current day repetitions and symptoms. Much of the work done with Mrs. C. involves what's called *reconstruction and construction*. In effect, this term refers to helping patients remember. For Mrs. C., it involved helping her to recall childhood events that made her vulnerable to the various symptoms and character problems with which she struggled.

As we worked together, I noticed how frequently she talked about the past. The past, and past problems with disappointments, hurts, and regular and routine empathic failures, stayed alive within her, coloring her sense of the world as a world of animals—animals that would hurt, hit, steal, grab, or seduce. The process of piecing together these parts of her history offered her much insight into her problems.

My work with Mrs. C. involved a great deal of construction and reconstruction. This work helped her to understand her *symptomatic feelings* of mistrust and her symptomatic belief that she should, therefore, stay away from people, since her world was a place of assault, intrusion, over-interest, and overstimulation. She developed a symptomatic alarm system set on perpetual "red alert" to deal with this, leaving her constantly on guard. All of this tension produced ongoing problems with people, headaches, chronic GI problems, and chronic sexual problems. I pointed out to her that she's always in a "clenched state." I observed this in her body positions: her arms are frequently tightly crossed over her body, clenching her arms with her hands. Her "kid" learned not to trust. Mrs. C.'s kid learned that people will hurt you, steal from you, cheat (as her father did in his business), and think only about themselves. The reconstruction of this perspective helped her to study her symptoms and gain better control over them.

C. experienced sex with the husband she loved and should trust as a dangerous and unwanted intrusion that must be carefully observed. This perspective interfered with her relaxation and prevented her from being comfortable. Her sexual symptoms were also complicated by the problems with her father: her history with her flirtatious, teasing, and narcissistic father led her to repeat teasing and flirtatiousness with others, as well as with me. I helped her see this pattern as she repeated and replayed it with me in the treatment and the transference. For example, she would say things such as, "You look great in blue." Our work with this pattern helped her to recall that one of the few gratifications of childhood was being admired and loved by her father. She helped to reproduce this all-too-rare good feeling by giving admiration back towards men. However, the conflictual oedipal wishes inherent in this behavior left her tense, guilty, and vulnerable to self-hurt. All of these issues improved as she learned more and more about herself and her history.

CHAPTER TWELVE

Patient D.: Understanding the repetition compulsion and unconscious fantasy

D. was a 35-year-old married physician who came to treatment because of multiple symptoms. He was intermittently depressed, anxious, and disgruntled about his life. He smoked marijuana frequently to deal with these feelings. He had few friends. D. left certain seemingly successful positions suddenly and impulsively, and had a history of doing the same kind of thing with girlfriends before his marriage. D. had cogent and intelligent explanations for these events that somehow seemed glib and not fully explanatory.

D.'s mother had died in a car accident when he was an early adolescent. Since then, he routinely battled with his demanding and pugnacious father, with whom he often felt at war.

One particularly dramatic episode occurred during this man's treatment that helped me to learn about trauma and, in particular, a fascinating and confusing mental phenomenon known as the repetition compulsion.

Early on, D. began to complain about the treatment. He felt it wasn't working and wanted to leave the treatment. I was aware of his past predilection to leave what seemed to me to have been good jobs and good relationships. I wasn't surprised that this issue had arisen in the treatment, but I was confused by it.

During certain sessions, some of the multiple determinants of this terribly self-destructive phenomenon revealed themselves to me in a way I've never forgotten. I hope they will elucidate for the reader new insights about the way the mind works.

At one point, D. described feeling pressured at work; he told me how "pent up" he had been recently. In one session, he started with the comment, "I feel like I'm going 90 miles an hour and ready to crash. I've been so pressured and working intensely. I just feel like I'm speeding at 90 miles an hour."

The words "hit" me and reminded me of one of the most seriously traumatic parts of D.'s background, namely his mother's car accident. When he repeated to me the "going 90 miles an hour" I asked him if the words reminded *him* of anything.

He said, "No," but he continued, "I feel out of control. I feel like I'm just speeding."

Once again I asked him if this reminded him of anything.

At that point he said hesitantly, "The accident?"

As it dawned on me, I told him that I thought he had been identifying with his mother in the act of her death. I told him he had been crashing jobs, smashing relationships and, most recently, seemed tempted to crash and smash the treatment.

In this particular dramatic point in treatment, the words "going 90 miles an hour and ready to crash," provided the clue about D.'s unconscious. I was also internally and affectively aware within myself of something sudden and bad about to happen. I felt quite involved in the treatment, and I had had a sense that the treatment was suddenly about to crash and burn.

D. began to remember details about the actual car accident at this point in the treatment. His mother had been driving a car that turned out to need a recall: it had a defective engine mount that caused the engine suddenly to drop, causing the car to shoot forward and hit a building, killing her.

What I began to interpret to D. over the course of many sessions is that he had become identified with her in the act of her death. He would cause jobs, relationships, and now the treatment suddenly to crash and burn. "Crash and bash" became part of our mutual lingo as we understood together the importance of these themes and how they had become unconsciously reenacted.

The way I understand it, the repetition compulsion is a human need to repeat and replay overwhelming, upsetting, uncontrollable aspects of our background over and over. D.'s repetitive destruction of relationships and situations was his way of "remembering." This case reminds me of one of Freud's observations: *What doesn't get remembered gets repeated.*

D.'s case also highlights another aspect of unconscious functioning that we've discussed before: *We tend to do unto others what's been done unto us.* As said, the unconscious is primitive; it is a part of the mind that follows Hammurabi's Code, Talion Law: "An eye for an eye, a tooth for a tooth," or even a death for a death.

As part of this repetition, D. did unto others what had been done unto him through his mother's death—he left. He left women, left employers, and was about to leave me and the treatment. He left different people in different ways—ways that were sudden and bewildering—leaving the other person dumbfounded and dumbstruck, the way D. himself had felt when his mother died, which he described as feeling that he was "walking in a cloud." Depersonalized, sad, anxious, and confused, his current victims must have felt similarly, as I also initially felt before I understood more about what was being repeated, replayed, and reenacted.

As D. and I explored all of this, including *reconstructing* what had happened, other interesting details involving the repetition and repetition compulsion emerged. For example, he told me that he drove a car that *Consumer Reports* labeled "the most dangerous car on the road."

My insight about his repetition of what his mother did in her dying came from multiple sources. The similarity of the words, his temptation to "crash" the treatment, the tension of what he was producing in me—i.e., the notion of a sudden ending and some awareness of what he might be repeating—began to come to my mind as I produced an interpretation.

Unconscious fantasy

The role of unconscious fantasy is also quite evident in this case. Dr. D. had been traumatized by his mother's death and the very traumatic circumstances surrounding it. Unconscious fantasy about her and her death was part of his dramatic and self-destructive symptoms and symptomatic enactments. Oddly and interestingly, the fantasy of being her, including being her in the act of her death, was for him a central unconscious fantasy.

In another episode, he told me of a fight that had occurred with his father not long after the accident. After the fight, Dr. D. climbed a tree and stayed there for a long while; he noted that he wanted to scare his father with another sudden absence. But he also referred to this scene on other occasions and asked out loud, "Why did I do that?"

When I said, "You'd be closer to heaven," he began to cry. Once again, the presence of an unconscious fantasy, i.e., being close to his mother in heaven, had dictated his behavior; realizing this concept helped both of us to understand the meaning of his odd, self-destructive, symptomatic actions. Once again, the unconscious fantasy of being near her, being with her, or actually being her, seemed to have been operating. The unconscious fantasy of joining her could also have been realized and enacted by falling out of that tree.

One of the exciting and gratifying parts of the work we do involves unearthing unconscious fantasy. It is a central ingredient in our mental lives and a very important aspect of working out symptoms and character problems with our patients.

Unconscious fantasy is revealed in innumerable ways. As we discussed early on in the text, the therapeutic analytic situation, together with the regression it fosters, is intended to allow us access to the unconscious. As we gain more access through the regression, unconscious fantasy begins to be revealed. Such revelation may begin with just a wisp of a thought on our part. At times we can become aware of unconscious fantasy in a sudden flash, as when Dr. D.'s threat of sudden departure "hit me". The more we sit with patients, the more these unconscious fantasies reveal themselves to us through symptoms, slips, dreams, associations, and enactments. The unearthing and understanding of unconscious fantasy is one of the most important, exciting, and therapeutic parts of being a psychotherapist.

What I've been describing also highlights the importance of trauma in mental life. I've found that trauma is often dealt with by repetition and identification. In D.'s case, he unconsciously repeated the act of his mother's dying over and over; endless conflicts led to endless endings. Getting "high" by smoking marijuana was another way of getting closer to heaven, anesthetizing himself, and expressing his rage.

Working through

It was only through the development of insight achieved over many years of work that Dr. D. understood and mastered these neurotic patterns. His understanding needed to be expanded and reunderstood in multiple ways. The term for this process, which comprises a great deal of work during a treatment, is called *working through*. I believe a version of this is needed in the learning process, one reason why I'm repeating certain themes throughout this text. After many of these insights occurred frequently, they became integrated for D., producing the result we seek: *Where id was, ego shall be.*

I believe that during Dr. D.'s phase of wanting to discontinue the treatment, the therapeutic alliance was part of what prevented a treatment "car wreck." The alliance we had developed helped him to stay with me as we continued our therapeutic journey, despite his very real and strong desire to smash the treatment in yet another version of a car crash that he had instigated and initiated many times before. Gradually, the treatment got back on track, and he remained in it despite, at times, strong temptations and inclinations to crash the treatment again and again.

In unraveling the strands of the rope and unearthing the relics of our dig, symptoms begin to give way and patients both feel better and get better. Through these insights, occurring over many years, D. became a far less self-destructive, destructive, and impulsive man. He became a more mature man. He told me that he felt the treatment had saved his life.

CHAPTER THIRTEEN

Patient E.: Giving patients new insights about common themes

In many treatments, certain common themes with which people need help emerge. For example, human beings struggle with impulses. Helping people to use *thought before action* is an oft-encountered need.

Mr. E, a successful restaurateur, who we talked about earlier in the text, came to treatment because of marital problems. E. had been married for about ten years; he had three young children and a very successful restaurant empire. He presented for treatment after he admitted to his wife that he had had an affair with a woman in the small community in which they lived.

While telling me about his situation, he quickly told me that one night, without giving it much thought, he decided "to get it off my chest with my wife." He said that his wife had been suspecting this affair from various clues she had obtained, and that she had badgered him and "interrogated" him about it. One night he thought, "Oh, just admit it—maybe it'll get her off my back." Impulsively, at that moment, he told her.

His wife was enraged. Her suspicions now confirmed, she launched into a withering, lengthy attack on him, directing verbal abuse toward him, speaking abusively about him to his children, and telling disparaging stories about him to her friends in the community. Her attacks grew relentless, despite attempts at marital treatment. Ultimately, he left and began living alone in a city apartment. She initiated divorce proceedings. E. was left with a sense of, "What happened?" as well as, "I thought I loved her," and, "How could it have come to this?"

The answers to these questions lay in behaviors and problems that had been in place for many years. Since E. was a teenager, he had flirted with the girlfriends of his own friends, at times even engaging them in some kind of "light" sexual activity. After he got married, he described going to school events for his children, "to check out the new hot mommas."

One of E.'s multiple problems was a problem with *grandiosity*, which took the form of the feeling, "You know, somehow I'll always end up okay." Denial is frequently a part of grandiosity. In this case, E. felt that he was leading "a charmed life" in which no harm would come to him—and if it did, it would quickly dissipate. One of the important elements of E.'s grandiosity lay in his identification with his own philandering father, a well-known figure in the community who had had multiple affairs, some of which he exhibitionistically revealed to his son. For example, he showed E. expensive jewelry he had purchased for one of his girlfriends. His father lived an active and, at times, impulsive life. This included sustaining a sports injury by recklessly engaging in something akin to playing football while skiing down a mountain. His life ended with what might have been a stroke (connected, significantly, to that sports injury) while in bed with a mistress, as his third marriage was failing.

One of the first tasks in E.'s treatment was pointing out the themes that emerged and were intimately interwoven—*impulsiveness, grandiosity,* and *masochism*.

E. wasn't sure he wanted his marriage to end. Nevertheless, his impulsive behavior, his affairs, and his sudden impulsive confession had caused it to end abruptly and badly.

E.'s story is hardly unique. Impulsiveness, in and of itself, without the other issues involved in E.'s situation, can take an infinite number of forms, ranging from sudden violence, drug use and abuse, and sudden sexual enactments with or without appropriate protection, to some of the most common maladies human beings experience, such as overeating. Impulses come in all shapes, sizes, and colors. Helping patients to put *thought before action* assists in working with another universal theme, namely, *masochism*.

The symptoms, inhibitions, and character problems that cause people to arrive at our offices often contain elements of self-hurtfulness. This tendency arises from the compromise formation of drive, defense, and conscience (punishment) that comprises symptoms and character pathology. *Helping people to see the ways in which they hurt themselves* can offer a beginning in the process of engaging them in a treatment.

It's frequently surprising and confusing to people that they are being self-hurtful, and yet it becomes readily apparent as we help them to examine the symptoms and modes of their functioning.

Returning to E., his impulsiveness was interwoven with his self-hurtfulness and grandiosity. His impulsiveness took the form not only of flirting or poorly-thought-out, swift sexual encounters; it also took various other forms. E. had earned millions of dollars over many years through his business. As he tackled his financial situation during the divorce proceedings, however, it appeared that he had saved relatively little of it. As he put it, he had "burned through it," and wasn't exactly sure how that had happened. E. didn't want to look at his financial situation. During some years he had made millions of dollars; during others, he had earned hundreds of thousands. He rarely knew how much he was making, and stayed away from important financial details. He also never kept track of his expenses.

In one session he told me, "I just found $500,000 in some account I forgot about." I pointed out to him that one problem with finding $500,000 is that you can also lose $500,000 and not know it. I spoke with E. about this side of his self-hurtfulness while staying away from technical words like "masochism," since speaking simply discourages intellectualization. Once again, the denial aspect of his grandiosity had allowed him to think he could get away with anything, and had prevented him from being aware of financial pitfalls. This included the narcissistic blow to the unconscious fantasy that he was infinitely wealthy.

Working with E.'s chronic problems with self-hurtfulness and impulsiveness became much more easily accomplished when I could show him the patterns, which kept on repeating themselves. *A neurosis is like a broken record; it just keeps going and going until someone sees what's going on.* The more E. saw the patterns repeating themselves in all their different colors, shapes, and sizes, the more he learned. And the more he learned, the more insight he developed. As I learned, he learned. That is how treatment works.

Symptoms are fueled by gratification

Both patient and therapist also learn that all symptoms and character problems are fueled by gratification. The unconscious works through wishes (gratifications). As we discover the multiple unconscious wishes that fuel symptoms and character problems, patients learn and grow. They become, like E., less impulse-ridden, less self-destructive.

As E. learned about his symptoms and character problems, he was able to recognize certain wishes that had been unconscious and were becoming more conscious. For example, like his philandering father, with whom E. identified, E. wished to be desired by all women. He also wished to be infinitely wealthy. His character problems betrayed these wishes and fantasies that were made conscious over the course of time, in the treatment.

As we discussed earlier in the text, another of E.'s symptomatic patterns was "Stu and Alan syndrome." This pattern involved his saying "yes" to mutually exclusive plans, people, etc., It gratified the wish to "have it all" and never exclude anything as a possibility. The process of trying to have it all produced another serious symptom that Mr. E. had, namely, a problem with honesty. Honesty was sacrificed and made secondary to promising simultaneous plans, affairs, and other behaviors. The childhood wishes of never having to make a choice, and thus never having to sustain loss, were some of the wishes that fueled his symptom with dishonesty.

We work preconsciously

We worked with E.'s unconscious wishes not by diving too deeply into the unconscious—"You want to kill your father and marry your mother"—but by working with the derivatives of those wishes closer to consciousness that lie just around the corner.

E. could *feel* his wish to keep going after women, even while trying to make his badly damaged marriage work. He could begin to *feel* that by not knowing how much money he actually had, he could preserve his wish to be endlessly wealthy. As these feelings became almost *palpable* we could address them more effectively. He discovered the identifications and other elements that were part of his oedipal and narcissistic pathology. With these discoveries, he slowly began to function in a more mature way.

Amidst the fascinating discovery of the complexities of these previously unconscious themes and fantasies, people become interested in themselves. Part of your work as a therapist is helping patients to join you as co-detectives in the fascinating process of their self-discovery. As their curiosity grows, their understanding grows. Simultaneously, a treatment and a treatment team grow, too.

CHAPTER FOURTEEN

Patient F.: Working with dreams

I enjoy working with dreams. My guess is that this comes across—and it may stimulate my patients to bring in dreams more frequently.

Freud spoke of dreams as being "the royal road to the unconscious," an issue that has been a subject of debate over the decades. Some have felt that dreams are of no greater or lesser importance than any other association patients have in helping us learn about themselves and their unconscious. Personally, I find that, at times, dreams have a unique power to illuminate the unconscious dramatically and curiously. These "movies of the mind" are written, directed, and produced by the dreamer, and we can derive a great deal from them to learn more about the dreamer in our work as therapists. For beginning therapists, dreams can be confusing and bewildering, leaving the novice asking, "What am I supposed to do with this?" The answer to that question is the subject of this section.

One place to begin our understanding of dreams is the initial insight that Freud had regarding dreams in his *piéce de résistance*, *The Interpretation of Dreams* (1900a). One of his first major insights was that dreams are the fulfillment of a wish. The unconscious is composed of wishes seeking discharge, and one way of expressing these wishes is disguised in a dream. I've found that dreams are not limited to the expression of a single wish; rather, they can express multiple wishes. What follows is a session in which a dream plays a very prominent role. My purpose in writing about this session is not only to expand your understanding of dreams, but also to point out how they become woven into the fabric of a treatment, how you can work with them to deepen a treatment, and how dreams can allow you, as a therapist, to understand, and thereby intervene, with greater clarity. By understanding a dream, I'm able to help patients understand more about themselves and continue to achieve greater mastery over their unconscious motivations.

The session being presented here took place several years into a treatment. I present it to give the reader a beginning appreciation for the way in which early work with a patient paves the way towards deeper insight for patient and therapist alike. The dreamer, Dr. F., a medical school anatomy instructor, presented with multiple symptoms, including great difficulty getting along with his wife, as well as provocatively oppositional behavior towards his students and fellow instructors. He had serious problems with procrastination, jeopardizing his career, and displayed an obsessive concern with detail that bogged him down in his work. At times he also experienced "confusional episodes" associated with much anxiety. He was having difficulty in finishing the treatment.

To provide my sense of what happened during this session, which is presented in dialogue format, I will relate my own reflections about the patient and myself in italics.

"P" is the patient, Dr. F. "T" is the therapist.

The session: After saying hello, I'm initially silent, allowing for a regression to take place and for the patient to go wherever his thoughts take him.

P: I had a dream that I forgot to tell you about. It was early Sunday morning. There's so much about dreams that I don't understand, and I barely understand the significance. I know it helps, being in touch with the unconscious, the subconscious, my slips. I have so much trouble remembering dreams, and I've been working at it—trying to—thinking I've been working on it. I remember nothing about the dreams I had last night. But what happened Sunday morning when I woke up, about 6 or 6:30 ... the dream was vividly in my mind. The whole dream was in my mind. I can't usually remember even a little snippet of a dream. Last night I went to the bathroom four times—maybe five times—and each time I woke up with a dream. But just coming back from the bathroom I had no idea what it was, what I was dreaming. I don't really know what I'm saying. I guess what I'm talking about is my puzzlement about the way my mind works. Why it's so unusual that I remembered the whole dream. There was a paper nearby and I just wrote it all down. And, until I looked at it, I could have told you absolutely nothing about it. I remember nothing at all. But when I started reading it, not only did it come back to me—much [of it], but not all of it, because there are some details in here that I don't remember at all—but I remember some of the imagery in more detail than I wrote down. [Pause] This one is strange. [Pause]

I'm aware of feeling struck by the lengthy preamble. Dr. F. came to treatment because of multiple symptoms. He wasn't comfortable with himself or with other people. He was frightened of people and had a serious self-esteem problem. The intellectualization is defensive and self-protective. I was also aware of some irritation on my part—I felt that he was "teasing me" by not getting to the dream. In the treatment, we've been talking about his "stalling" as a way of his expressing his fearfulness and carefulness, as well as a passive-aggressive element.

T: I can't help wondering whether some of this preamble involves the stalling we've been discussing. Are you "doing your thing," as we've been talking about?

P: I hear you. I don't think so. I'm trying to express, you know, I was thinking about it and I let you know about the dream. You may call it stalling. I would call it trying to glean more understanding about your perspective about dreams. Before I open this up to read it, I was remembering a comment you made about a dream. It was very interesting to me. As you know, I'm still watching for signals—indication from the other—so I think it's fair to assume that here I would be especially sensitive to you. I think that's what these comments have been all about—trying to make sense of you—and I don't know if you want to tell me your sense of significant dreams. Or your attitude towards dreams, or whatever. And also the nature of dreams themselves.

T: I understand, but what else might you be doing?

I believe he's "doing" various things. He is excessively worried about criticism, including from me, and is continuing to guard against it by intellectualizing. I'm aware that it's preventing him, and us as a treatment team, from progressing. I'm also trying to help him observe what he's "doing."

P: I do have an intellectual interest in dreams and, I should say, their meaning or significance.

T: I also wonder, as we've been talking about it, whether you may not be hearing today how you're choosing your words so carefully—I think that even that kind of intellectual playing with words could be another way of doing the stalling, perhaps a self-consciousness about being wrong.

With this intervention, I'm trying to interpret more directly what I think is happening. One of Dr. F.'s important symptoms is procrastination—"He doesn't get there." He procrastinates seriously, outside and inside the treatment. I'm trying to help him self-observe this.

P: I don't know. That's possible. I mean, I've always felt very inadequate when it comes to this, so I've been surprised to realize that my way of talking is very intellectual. But you're right, as you describe it. I want to make sure that I mean what I say and say what I mean. What am I debating against? Being wrong? Yes, that. But it's also being thought stupid, and I'm always ... talk about covering up—what's the word I'm looking for—trying to hide something from people. You know I'm big on malaprops, for example. And I'm constantly—you've heard the expression—putting my foot in my mouth. It's so with me. Because it's something I feel about myself. If I'm not careful, I'm going to put my foot in my mouth. Not here, but outside of here. And so I usually don't say anything. Not so true now. You know. But still, the opposite is not true now, either. I'm debating against the other person, wishing they weren't with me.

I'm aware of thinking about his arguing symptom and his symptomatic detachment from people.

P: I guess that's the best way of putting it. And there's a lot of that feeling in last Thursday's session. I came back feeling that all of them wished I were not there—Z surely wished I was not involved. So I don't think what you witnessed in me is stalling, so much as I don't know how ... I guess I'm trying to make sense of a larger picture. It's interesting you used the word "stalling," because it's my sense that you don't really care whether the dream is discussed or not. It's my opinion—no real sense—that you can do your work, and help me do mine, with this dream or without it.

T: That's interesting, but I do think there's been some stalling about this dream.
P: I was ready to do it two days ago.
T: Yet, why didn't you?
P: I don't remember what we were talking about. I think some of those things were and the way I ... what am I defending against? There seems something very silly about this dream. And at the same time something very apparent about the dream, almost obvious—too obvious.
T: Perhaps that's a clue. I think you don't want to be either silly or transparent.

Once again, what's closest to the surface—and thus easier to interpret here—is his self-esteem vulnerability, which I have mentioned.

P: I have no trouble with silly. But transparent is really quite interesting. Outside of here, it's absolutely true. I do not want people to see into me, to know what's really going on.
T: I think that gives us a new understanding of your term "treading water." I think that treading water is stalling. Using lots and lots of words prevents you from being seen through.
P: That's quite conscious. When I go to treading water mode, I am quite consciously hiding my innermost thoughts—working very hard to hide what I'm thinking or feeling from anybody around me. And indeed, that's exactly what I mean by treading water, as opposed to swimming ahead.
T: I think that could even be true during those moments in here, in the treatment, when you don't know what to talk about or where you debate and hesitate.
P: But then again, the question is, "What am I afraid of?" And let's leave the issue we call "the stall." When I get to the dream—and

it's funny, I was reading my notes; they're hard to read, 'cause I wrote it when I was half asleep. To some degree I can identify, 'cause I remember it well. I think it says, "It's marathon day. It's marathon day in the town where I live. I had intended to run in this marathon. I was in shape for it, but I missed it. So, I joined the race. In other words, I got in the race anyway. But I was dressed in my heavy winter coat—(almost) a parka." The almost is in parentheses. "It was dark out, maybe. I had trouble with the route. I could picture it in my mind. In fact, in the dream—now, I've been in four marathons, and the marathon in the dream was nothing like an actual marathon. These were not wide roads at all. There were not thousands of people. There were just a number of runners. They were never paired, in fact. They were running in a sort of file." The runners were tall, lanky, athletic. That's not in here, but that's my memory. Sometimes I was sure I was on the route. Other times I saw the runners near the finish. Then I wrote down here, "Was I running it backwards?" In other words, it seemed to me that they were running in one direction—all of them—and I was running in the opposite direction. They were passing me. Again, [I was] dressed in this clunky way and they were dressed rather sleekly—sleeveless top, running shorts, socks, and shoes. At some point I realized I had stopped. Was I in a bathroom stall? To look at something? 'Cause I no longer had my shoes on, but what I wrote is, "my front-seat casual shoes." I knew exactly which shoes I had had on. Not these. I had ones—they're black. They're sneaker soles, but they have leather tops. I did not have my running shoes. So I thought I didn't have those shoes on, and it was hard to run, so I tried to retrace my steps to find where I had put down my shoes. The implication being: nowhere in the dream do I remember taking them off. But clearly I had had them on and now I did not have them on, so I must have taken them off. But I couldn't remember exactly where I had been. I couldn't find the route.

And that's the whole dream. You probably go into town often enough, and when builders are doing work they put up what's called a bridge—now it's scaffolding—and people walk under the scaffolding. And in the writing I referred to it being dark. What I meant was that I couldn't see daylight because these runners were running under that kind of scaffolding ... again, in one direction, and I was running in the other direction—with that parka on. And that's the whole dream. And what do I think it's about? In a lot of ways it's about the treatment.

T: The treatment must feel like a marathon.

One technique involved in working with dreams is for the therapist to allow himself to associate as he listens to a dream and monitor those associations. Indeed, one thought I had as I listened to the dream was that the treatment, which was taking a long time, felt like a marathon, perhaps to both of us.

However, there are other contexts for the dream, as we've discussed earlier, including the patient's past and current reality outside the treatment.

P: Yes, and also what we were just talking about before I read the dream. In my not knowing what to talk about, I don't know where I'm going. I don't know how to get there.

The associations that precede a dream are associations to the dream. Indeed, it seems as if some of those themes—i.e., "getting there or not"— did precede the telling of the dream and are very relevant in understanding the dream, as Dr. F. observes.

T: At one point you don't know where you are, but you realize you're in a *stall*. How about that word?

The unconscious double meaning of a word frequently occurs, providing further clues about the unconscious.

P: You mean that I was stalling? That I actually stopped running at that moment? I was in a stall. Here I had this dream last Saturday night into Sunday morning, but we've talked about stalling in the last number of weeks or months. It's that part of me that feels now like the therapy is racing ahead. I feel like I am doing better in the last couple of years, in spite of what I experienced last Thursday and Friday, than in a long time. Or certainly the past several years. I feel much more in command of myself, in general. What was it—three weeks ago, now?—that Friday, when I spent fifteen minutes of anecdoting and then said I don't know what to talk about? And you made that comment that I hadn't noticed my stalling. You call it stalling, and I'm not objecting, but I am saying that, to me, it feels genuinely like I don't know what to talk about. The race metaphor—the running metaphor—running is something that I like, and [it] probably also reflects a wish to get back to running. It's never going to happen, but the wish is there. [Pause] Let's see, going in the opposite direction, wearing all the wrong clothes, missing it ...

T: Such an important child side phenomenon. Like the chastised one, late for school.

I bring it back to his past, to a story, well-known to both of us, that seems connected to the dream. Dr. F. had, in early childhood, been chronically late for school. This would enrage his mother, who would yell at him for his lateness and for other behaviors like it. This lateness was part of a broader sado-masochistic problem with his irritable, embittered mother, who was chronically angry at him and that is repeated regularly professionally. He was chronically angry at her in kind, but dealt with his own anger in endless passive and passive-aggressive ways. In this particular story, he went to school so early that no one was in the school yard. Confused and frightened, he decided to go home again.

P: You know, that was part of the image—when I said I was going in one direction, the others going in the other direction. What I remember—again, this was the time that I was on time for school. And I describe it so often, because when I got to school, the school yard was empty. Going back home, and all these kids coming to school, and my yelling at them that they were late.

T: And how do we understand your befuddlement?

P: Well, it's really terror, you see. I was so terrified.

T: It seems you were terrified of something else, as well. I think you were terrified of your defiance. Terrified of your urge to go against the crowd, to go against her. She wanted you there on time. Howard (his childhood nickname) didn't know that he wanted to oppose her. All he could do was to get into this befuddled state—get there overly early, come home, and risk being late in the process. He wasn't aware of this wish to oppose. But he was terrified of being caught at his secret opposition—his secret staying at the movie theater, his secret playing at the train tracks, and his secret being late for school. Mom would get very angry. The only thing he could do was to become a staller, not even knowing what the stalling was about, fooling himself.

The dream helps to further make conscious certain events and themes (passive aggressiveness) and their role in the sado-masochistic relationship he had with his mother. The dream also elucidates the existence of the same problem, outside and inside the treatment.

P: You're saying the stalling goes back to that. It's interesting how you described the terror, because I often find myself in a befuddling situation, which, for me, is scary. I have a sense that other people would know what to do or how to deal with a situation, and I'm going to show my own inadequacy. I can remember getting to that school yard and seeing it empty. Why I thought that I was late, I can't understand. That was first grade. So that would make me—I turned five in March of kindergarten—so I was five and a half. And, I mean—I don't know—I doubt very much that I could tell time. And I know many second-graders, seven-year-olds, cannot. So I was five and a half and, to me, that play yard was empty when I got there. My mother said—I remember before I left for school that morning, so afraid that I was going to be late—my mother said, "You know you're going to be there in plenty of time. Now, go." I went and saw no kids on the way. I got there, and the playground was empty. I was sure I was in for it, another scolding like I had gotten the day before. I was afraid to go up to anybody to ask them—to go into the building—and I ran home. And I do remember. But now I was in such a state of terror, worrying that I would be late again. I didn't trust what my eyes were seeing—that so many kids were coming to school. And again I got home, and my mother sent me right back, and I made it to the school on time. That's how early I had been. It reminds me of the time I got to your office, when I got there before you did. I wasn't worried then. But the other side—you know, something else you said, "What about the wish? The wish to stall?" I can remember the panic. It's really amazing. You know, 35 years later, I can still remember the panic and fear I felt on the playground ... in a certain sense that panic sort of set in, this sense of befuddlement, of not knowing how to deal with situations.

T: You had to befuddle yourself to not know about your wish to oppose.

In previous weeks and months we had been doing much therapeutic work on his secret anger and secret oppositionalism. This work paved the way for my interventions, and may have been another context for the dream itself.

P: Well, I didn't trust my mother. I didn't trust anybody.
T: You didn't trust anybody, and you were angry at everybody—angry at the crowd. That's one reason you became a crowd "go againster".
P: That is so complicated, what you're saying. That brings in all kinds of memories and thoughts. This is what I'm doing—how I disagree with everybody (*one of the issues that brought him to treatment*), with what they're doing. You're saying that it's because I'm angry at everybody. And I can't say that that's not reasonable. But, in my work, I can say that I think they're doing it wrong. [Pause]
T: There's another important theme in this dream that deserves to be looked at, perhaps something you didn't think I was going to want to hear. Your comment regarding the dream being about the treatment—in what way are you doing it here? Are you going against the flow in here? In what way are you running the wrong way in here in this marathon treatment?
P: There was some of that—again, going back—that was a very important Friday that took place three weeks ago tomorrow. I'm talking about, not the first fifteen minutes, but the period that I said that I was totally confused. I did not know what to talk about. It connects to everything we're talking about today, even that Friday. Almost from the beginning of the treatment, I got the sense that you expect me to know what I'm supposed to be doing. Right from the beginning, you set those guidelines very early in the treatment and then ... go to it. I'm supposed to go to it. It reminds me of the starting gun. It reminds me of something that happened very early in my treatment with Dr. Y., and I'm almost certain I described this more than once. And this was on—real early—I don't really remember, but I want to say, certainly, within the first two years, maybe the first two months. And that is, I came in and, after I finally got going, I said I didn't

know what to talk about, and that he already heard everything that I have to talk about. Of course, I know now that he hadn't, but what was on my mind at the time were things I had already said and all I could do was repeat those things. Now I've learned a huge amount—and that is, not only is it OK to repeat, but some of the work that gets done in therapy is from repetition. But in the repeating, the feeling for me is that I'm boring you. Again, certainly one of my constants—and I don't know if it's a fear or wish ... "a wish," I say, because I've learned here that I believe people would find me unsatisfactory to be with ... that people would not want to be with me. Maybe it's a wish—to have people not want to be with me. It's hard to understand. What's occurring to me now is I'm trying to get even with my mother through everybody else.

T: "Everybody else." In other words, without even knowing it, you're being the opposer. The starting gun sounds, and what happens? Running around in circles. Going the opposite way.

P: In this dream, I wasn't even there with the starting gun. I had totally forgotten that this was marathon day, and I only realized it when I saw the runners. And, dressed as I was, I just joined the race, sometimes running in the right direction, sometimes not. That reminds me, you know, you know I get—I've talked about this—there's a painful feeling, but I get so upset when people criticize me.

As I reread the session, I also realized that he was expressing his ambivalence about joining the "human race," which I could have mentioned, but didn't think of at the time.

P: The image that I'm remembering now—this must have been two years ago, probably in the spring or summer—I was running in the park. That's how I know it can't be that long ago; we only had the apartment for two years. And I came across a race in the park. And it was women running. But I'm not sure whether I realized that or not. *(He's also had gender identity problems.)* But I started running with them because racers provide or offer challenge. In other words, there is so much more incentive to run faster when I'm in a race. So I joined the race. I also remember the other times when I was running in the wrong direction against the runners—in reality. In the park, it's a wide road, and I'm not alone. There are plenty of people who do this kind of thing. But I am super, super, super conscientious about doing it right. And you're supposed to run it in a certain direction and walk in a certain direction and I've never done it otherwise. But so many people do. And I say, "Don't they read the sign? What's the matter with these people?" My point that I'm trying to get to, though, is that once—here's this women's race—somebody said to me, "You're not supposed to be in this race." Well, I didn't realize that I wasn't supposed to be doing what I was doing. It was like when somebody honks at me because I'm doing the wrong thing in the car. Or sometimes they just get angry because they're just being impatient. It's very hard. What I'm trying to say is, it's very hard for me to deal with these kinds of situations.

T: I would say that it really represents a wish to express a rage that you have felt against the world. You go against the world the way Howard did. It reminds me of what I was pointing out to you with words—with fastidiousness about words. On the one hand, with the word thing, you're being super-fastidious. You're being super-conscientious in here as a patient, being very careful, which you are. You're taking the treatment very seriously and trying to be very conscientious and careful as you go through this. On the other hand, you're unwittingly stalling, so that you don't get there—so that you don't get to the end of the race in here, as well. You can imagine what it would be like if you spent an entire session questioning words. The fastidiousness, in and of itself, becomes the obstacle—becomes the running circles, the quality that you're describing in the dream. You could run in circles with words, *using words* as your route to satisfying the childhood wish of staying the child forever.

P: With you taking care of me forever.

T: The wish to never finish here, to never finish this marathon treatment.

P: I see that. In here, I'm trying to say it right, but outside of here I don't want to say it at all.

T: You're worried about putting your foot in your mouth, which has to do with expressing anger more directly. But here you can see how your use of words represents so much. It also involves a wish to hang on to me, a wish to not get to the finish line, the wish to oppose, to not get there. Just make this into an intellectual exercise. This dream is a helpful one. And so, I'm interested to hear your comment that you're not sure that I value dreams. It has that bewildered, oppositional quality to it. I don't doubt that you mean that, but I think it's in line with this whole thing.

Many of my interventions are based on previous work that we've done. I would not be able to so directly interpret many of these wishes—to express anger, to oppose, or to stay with me—without the previous work we had done on these issues. But the dream consolidates them, clarifies them, and helps in working them out.

P: These are things I've seen a number of times in here—my wish not to change. And I know about the wish to hold on to you, because there is conscious ambivalence about finishing. I can identify with both parts of the ambivalence.

SECTION V

CONCLUSION

CHAPTER FIFTEEN

On endings

Dr. F., in the previous chapter, was making certain changes in his life and in the way he worked within the treatment. Profound shifts began to take place in his understanding of himself, which helped him to get a much better handle on his problems. He grew to know himself in certain basic and important ways that led to the development of real changes in the symptoms with which he had presented. He fought less with students and his wife; his self-esteem improved; and he felt happier and more comfortable. We decided that we had done enough work for him to be able to finish the treatment.

Finishing a treatment is always a relative phenomenon. Issues and problems always remain undone or partially finished. Many patients are able to work on these unfinished issues on their own, self-analytically, for as long as they need to, without the help of a formal, external therapist. As autonomy is the goal of every treatment, people generally need an opportunity to finish work with a therapist and forge ahead on their own. A notable exception might be those individuals with serious mental illnesses, who may need the ongoing support of an outside external therapist indefinitely.

It can be hard to know when patients are ready to finish. Of course, one of the indications of a treatment working and approaching an end point is improvement in the symptoms and inhibitions that bring people to us in the first place. It should lead to a person feeling more comfortable.

What follows is an account written by Florence, a 70-year-old woman who had come to see me because of marital problems and a pervasive feeling of unhappiness. She felt alone, inhibited, and stymied in her life. Her childhood had its share of unhappiness. There was a great deal of fighting between her belligerent, raging father and a troubled older brother which scared her into intimidated, frightened silence. Florence has been in once-a-week psychotherapy with me for about a year and as she states had never written about herself before:

The room

When I thought of it, it wasn't about the coldness of the therapy room or even that the room appeared what it was not to me, but that the inability to express my thoughts stymied me. Once I blurted out my thoughts about the room and about my perception of you, I felt better… and then realized that what seemed to be, really was not. But that admitting my feelings and then having dialogue was healthy.

I found you intimidating when I first started therapy. You were an austere figure of authority—kind of like my father—remote, unapproachable— You are not those things, but that is how I perceived you initially. I built up a wall around myself—I would not let you in. I guess you reminded me of other people who were very bright and who made me feel uncomfortable. I saw myself as less intelligent than you, and I felt uncomfortable, and then I retreated to that lonely place inside of myself. Only when I began to trust that you were really interested in helping me and were patient and understanding AND NON-JUDGMENTAL could I begin to open up to you and express my feelings. Writing my feelings is very unusual for me. But I find it is easy for me to analyse my feelings and reactions by writing. I feel that I am really beginning to make progress in changing my old patterns of behavior.

I am very pleased that I continued to come to therapy even when it was painful for me to be here. In the past I would stop things in mid-stream—be it with weight counselors, other psychotherapists, chiropractors—However, this time I persisted, became comfortable with expressing my opinions ... and there is no stopping me now!!! (at the moment, at least). In my heart I knew that it was now or never for me to recognize my problems and to work on them. I am hopeful that this is the right course for me—although my husband and friends doubted it was right for me. And now I believe it is a gift I am giving myself. I believe I can make peace with many issues if I face them and you and I work together to resolve them.

Then in another excerpt:

I awoke with a thought—I had such an exhilarating day—teaching so freely with such animation—I had the students in the palm of my hand—loving all my innovative projects—then my confrontation with the golf club's president when she pressed my buttons—then the wonderful time with an old friend and accepting her for who she is—It was ambrosia—there was a sense of release—the world seems kinder and friendlier—because that is how I feel—and I don't want the good feelings to end. In the past I would revert to negativity—and retreat from people as I had in my childhood. Whenever I couldn't deal with the situation in my home, I would retreat to my room—and would begin to feel very lonely—the silence and imprisonment was comforting, but scary. It is no surprise that I like to surround myself with people in group situations. It is more comfortable than being alone. Old patterns have a way of popping up again—retreating, not facing and resolving conflict and the ensuing frustration—I have no assurance that the old patterns will not return, but perhaps I am learning methods to deal with these issues—by attacking them, finding my voice and expressing my opinions, for better or for worse.

Florence seems to have captured and understood the transference reaction she was having toward me and in working it out she was freed up to become much more assertive with her husband and others in her life. The problems from childhood, which she discussed and then understood, led to a self esteem improvement as well.

In finding her voice, she wrote this poem about the treatment:

Learning to Dance

My dancing teacher is patient with me.
He observes me, guides me and encourages me.
Hesitantly I start to learn the steps. They are difficult.
But I listen to the music, feel the rhythm and pay attention.
Pay attention, pay attention, expanding my mind, I stay focused.
I take a few tentative steps. I hear the beat and follow his lead.

I practice, practice, practice.
I make many mistakes along the way.
But then with a spirit of adventure, I gather the courage
To try new patterns, change directions,
And let go of the old and the unbalanced.
I begin to feel comfortable with my new honed skills.
I LET GO.........AND I'M DANCING.

When either patient or therapist thinks that a time to end is approaching, I generally suggest that we do a clinical evaluation together. We look at the symptoms and problems that brought them to treatment, as well as the symptoms and problems of which they became aware during the treatment. We examine what their life is like, outside and inside the treatment. Have transference issues been relatively well resolved? Sometimes we decide we need to do more work on A or B, and we do that work prior to a formal termination. Sometimes we decide that we've done enough for the person to be comfortable and ready to pursue things, including self-analytic work, on their own. The treatment frequently prepares people to understand and develop new insights, and to make new connections—in short, to do self-analytic work on their own—as it seems to have with Florence. Once that is decided, we typically pick a termination date down the road, work toward it, and say goodbye.

Not infrequently, when a termination date has been picked, regressions may take place. Such regressions may serve as an unconscious way for patients to hang onto the treatment, and may reflect "the impingement of loss of a significant object" (Firestein, 1978, p. 211). Fenichel made note of "symptomatic worsening to spite the analyst who is not fulfilling transference wishes" (Fenichel, 1945, as cited in Firestein, 1978, p. 241). He goes on to reassure the therapist: "Fortunately in most instances this is short-lived" (Fenichel, 1945, as cited in Firestein, p. 241). I've generally found that this phenomenon is more frequent in analysis than in psychotherapy, but I believe it can happen in either setting.

Eventually Dr. F. (whose treatment was much longer than Florence's) and I felt that enough work had been done. We picked a termination date, worked toward it, and said goodbye. In his case, that termination period took months to reach, as his treatment had taken several years. I find that frequently, but not always, the length of a termination period correlates with the amount of time that a person has been in treatment. Enough time should be given to consolidate the insights and gains a person has made, and adequate time should be given to the patient to separate and say goodbye to the therapist. Work on separation issues can be particularly productive during a termination phase. The termination phase may also be quite helpful in elucidating and fleshing out insights that have occurred throughout the treatment.

It's hard to know, however, exactly when to stop or how much time is needed for a termination phase. Enough time should be given to work adequately on remaining symptoms, remaining questions, and lingering issues, as well as the separation itself, in order for termination to be useful and therapeutic. Termination shouldn't be too abrupt, nor should it be drawn out endlessly. There are times when, after a lengthy, meaningful treatment, it is hard for both participants to let go of each other. Nevertheless, at some point it needs to be done; the work must be continued by both parties on their own.

The process of helping those with whom we work to become more comfortable and mature varies in length, as with Florence and Dr. F., and each treatment has its own unique twists and turns. The process of learning about oneself continues after a formal treatment is over—continued insights develop on one's own. That development is a part of the process that has no ending.

There is simply no substitute in the learning process for sitting with patients over time; it is a crucial part of the process of learning to do psychotherapy. Our patients are our textbooks, and we learn by the seat of our pants (Rako & Mazer, 1980, p. 71).

I hope that this text has clarified certain beginning issues in conducting psychotherapy, and I also hope that it serves as a springboard for further learning. The learning continues throughout life for both participants in the therapeutic partnership. That is what makes our field such an exciting and creative challenge.

BIBLIOGRAPHY

Baranger, W. & Baranger, M. (1962). La situation analitica como campo dinamico. *Revista Uruguaya de Psicoanalisis*, 4: 3–54.

Bion, W.R. (1962). *Learning from Experience*. London: Tavistock.

Fenichel, O. (1945). *The Psychoanalytic Theory of Neurosis*. New York: Norton.

Firestein, S. (1978). *Termination in Psychoanalysis*. New York: International Universities Press, Inc.

Freud, S. (1900a). The Interpretation of Dreams. *Standard Edition, Volumes 4–5*.

Freud, S. (1912). Recommendations to Physicians Practising Psycho-Analysis. *Standard Edition, Volume 12*, 110.

Freud, S. (1916–1917g [1915]). Mourning and Melancholia. *Standard Edition, Volume 14*, 243–258.

Gladwell, M. (2005). *Blink: The Power of Thinking Without Thinking*. London & New York: Little, Brown & Co./Time Warner Book Group.

Jacobs, T. (Ed.) (1991). *The Use of the Self: Countertransference and Communication in the Analytic Situation*. Madison, CT: International Universities Press, Inc.

Langs, R. (Ed.) (1981). *Classics in Psychoanalytic Technique*. New York & London: Jason Aronson.

Lewis, J.M. (1978). *To Be a Therapist: The Teaching and Learning*. New York: Brunner/Mazel.

Moore, B. & Fine, B. (Eds.) (1990). *Psychoanalytic Terms and Concepts*. London & New Haven: The American Psychoanalytic Association & Yale University Press.

Rako, S. & Mazer, H. (Eds.) (1980). *Semrad: The Heart of a Therapist*. New York & London: Jason Aronson.

Winnicott, D.W. (1969). The use of an object. *International Journal of Psychoanalysis*. 50: 711–716.

*LYRIC ACKNOWLEDGMENT

Same Ole Love

Words and Music by Darryl Roberts and Marilyn McLeod
© 1986 JOBETE MUSIC CO., INC.

All Rights Controlled and Administered by EMI APRIL MUSIC INC.

All Rights Reserved International Copyright Secured Used by Permission.

INDEX

Abstinence 18
Advice-giving
   guidance 63
   therapist 22
Affection-starved child 73
Ambiguity 26–28
Analytic listening 47–49
Anonymity 18–19
Auschwitz 68
Automaton 68

Band camp 68
Bathroom encounters 70
Beginnings in Psychotherapy 5
Bleger, Jose 29
Blink 54
Brown-outs 76

Caraca, Mary 68
Clinical cases 65
   Patient A, educating
     about cure 67–73

Patient B, encouraging
   self-observation 75–80
Patient C, identifying
   themes and furthering
   understanding of how
   symptoms develop 81–85
Patient D, understanding
   the repetition compulsion
   and unconscious
   fantasy 87–91
Patient E, giving patients new
   insights about common
   themes 93–97
Patient F, working with
   dreams 99–111
Clinical psychologist 39
Confidentiality 23–24
Confusional episodes 100
Constancy and consistency 30
   environmental 31
   physical 31

Contiguity 59
Countertransference, therapist 20–21
Crash and bash 88

Delphic oracle 63
Demeanor 36
Deprivation 11–14

Educating about cure 67–73
Encouraging self-observation 75–80
Eichler 58
Ekman, Paul 54
Empathy 45–47
Mr. E.'s syndrome 60

Fastidiousness 110
Feminine identification 73
Fenichel 47
Frame 29–34
    handling missed sessions 33–34
    money 33
    physical office 30–33
    time 30
Free association 25
Free-associative process 41
Frequency and timelessness 24–25
Freud, Anna 21
Freud, Sigmund 8–9
    archeological metaphor 51
    helpful metaphors 72
    later explanation of cure 52
    topographic theory 51
Friesen, Wallace 54
Frustration-tolerance 70

GI problems 84
GI symptoms 81
Giving patients new insights about common themes 93–97
Gladwell, Malcolm 54
    Blink 54
Grandiosity 94

Gratifications 56
    of childhood 85
    symptoms are fueled by 96
Gratification
    and deprivation 11–14
    abstinence role 18
    balancing act 13
    cartoonish vignette 12
    example of balancing 13–14, 18
    examples 12
    treatment 12

Hammurabi's Code 32, 89
Heterosexual
    forays 68
    identity 67
Homophobic therapist 22
Homosexual
    dream 22
    enactment 69
    valet 72

Identifying themes and furthering understanding of how symptoms develop 81–85
Idiosyncratic 61
Impulse-control matured 70
Impulsiveness 94
Interactional elements 48
Interrogative detective work 57
Intervening 61–63
Intrusive thoughts 76, 80

Listening and intervening
    context and contiguity 58–59
    detective work 57
    educating about cure 51–52
    educating patients on their jobs 50–51
    educating the patient 49
    empathy 45–47
    "flight instructors" 49
    following the affect 54–55

INDEX

going after pain 56–57
guideposts 45
keeping self esteem in mind 56
learning to understand and
    cure 52–53
lecture and the lab 59–61
mental content, three areas 57–58
"off-key" notes 55
patterns 55–56
resistance 53–54
treatment as a listening focus 58
Listening focus 58

Making the unconscious conscious 51
Masculine identity 67
Masochism 94–95
Mental content, three areas 57–58
Monopoly® cards 77–78
Mourning and Melancholia 73
Mutuality 38

Neutrality 21
Neurotic compromises 83

"Off-key" notes 55
"Our patients are our textbooks" 65

Parents' relative paucity 73
Penis hunting 69–70
Phallic achievement 71
Police-like fact-gathering 57
Psychoanalysis
    fundamental rule of 25
    transference 19–20
Psychoanalysts 5, 36
Psychopharmacology 40
Psychotherapist
    blankness 35
    grotesque violation 36
    spontaneity 36
Psychotherapy
    abstinence 18
    advantages of 54

analytic listening 47–49
analytic therapeutic situation 29
anonymity 18
beginning therapists 4
beginnings 3–5
benefits 3
clinical cases 65
complex concepts 5
consultation 39–42
context and contiguity 58–59
cookbook 5
course of analytic 17
creating a therapeutic
    atmosphere 35–38
educating patients on their jobs
    50–51
educating the patient 49
empathy 45
following the affect 54–55
frame in 29–34
going after pain 56–57
insight-oriented 19
"insight-oriented" versus
    "supportive" 63
intervening 61–63
keeping self esteem in mind 56
learning to understand and
    cure 52–53
lecture and the lab 59–61
listening and intervening,
    guideposts for our
    work 45–63
mental content, three
    areas 57–58
mutuality 38
novice patients 49
NYU Medical Center 4
"off-key" notes 55
on endings 115–119
on gratification and
    deprivation 11–14
on regression and its use 17–28
own unconscious 9

patients 25
patterns 55–56
practicing 3
process 4
professional methodology 18
psychoanalytic 20
resistance 53–54
supportive 19
time 29
tools and techniques 15
treatment as a listening focus 58
unconscious meaning 7–8
understanding the unconscious 17
why we do what we do 7–9

Reconstruction and construction 84
Regression and use 17–28
    ambiguity 26–28
    confidentiality 23–24
    couch 28
    countertransference, therapist 20–21
    free association 25–26
    frequency and timelessness 24–25
    insight-oriented versus supportive approach 19
    neutrality 21–22
    safety and freedom 22–23
    silence 26
    transference 19–20

Sado-masochistic version of treatment 57
Safety and freedom 22
Scaffolding 104
SCID (Structured Clinical Interview for DSM IV) 38
Screwing 83
Self-destructive phenomenon 88
Self-listening task 51
Self-monitoring 48

Self-observation 50–51, 75
Self-punitive behaviors 61
Semrad, Elvin 11–12
Sexual abuse 72
Sexual activity
    "light" 94
Sexual situation and other symptoms 72
"Sleazy" business dealings 83
"Stu and Alan" behaviors outside the treatment 61
Stu and Alan syndrome 59–61, 96
Symptomatic
    attitude 83
    symptomatic
    feelings 84
    regression 77
    worsening 118
Symptoms and character problems 96

Talion Law 89
The Interpretation of Dreams 99
Therapeutic alliance 36–38
Therapeutic atmosphere 35–38
Transference 19–20
    rebelliousness 72
Transferential
    feelings and enactments 37
    reactions 26, 37
Traumatic day 67

Unconscious
    "radar" 48
    fantasy 89–91
    resistance 54
Understanding the repetition compulsion and unconscious fantasy 87–91
    working through 91

Working with dreams 99–111